TEACH YOURSELF BOOKS

CARPENTRY

This practical handbook on carpentry is intended both for the beginner and for the more experienced woodworker. It deals first with the
choice, use and care of tools, and then goes on to discuss the different
kinds of joints and their application, how to make doors and drawers,
fitting locks and hinges, veneering and wood finishing. The final three
chapters give designs and instructions for making a wide variety of
household and garden articles, ranging from spice racks and coffee
tables to greenhouses and worksheds. Metricated throughout, the text
is profusely illustrated with drawings and photographs.

Mr. Hayward gives you not only sound advice on tools and workshop practice, joints and their application, indoor and outdoor woodwork, but also the designs and instructions for the making of a number of useful things.

Ideal Home

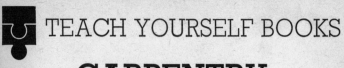

TEACH YOURSELF BOOKS

CARPENTRY

Charles Hayward

Formerly Editor of *The Woodworker*

ST. PAUL'S HOUSE WARWICK LANE LONDON EC4P 4AH

First printed 1939
Second edition 1960
Third edition 1969
Fourth edition 1973

ISBN 0 340 18049 8

Filmset in Photon Times 11 on 11½ pt. by
Richard Clay (The Chaucer Press), Ltd., Bungay, Suffolk
and printed in Great Britain by
Fletcher & Son, Ltd., Norwich

Contents

Preface

The desire to make things is inherent in most of us, and in accordance with our own particular make-up so we begin to make furniture, paint pictures, beat out metal, make model ships, or whatever it may be. Some crafts call for special ability in one direction or another, and if one does not happen to possess it the craft is ruled out entirely. Woodwork is almost unique in this connection, for there are very few people who cannot go in for it. This is partly because anyone, given intelligent application, can learn to work wood successfully and partly because there are so many branches of woodwork that practically everyone can find one that will appeal to him. Consider for a minute a few of the things that can be made: furniture, toys, garden woodwork, models, carving, general household woodwork, etc. A man's tastes must be very specialised if he cannot find something here to interest him.

There are other reasons, however, why woodwork is the ideal hobby. It is inexpensive, the material being comparatively cheap and the tools not costly (many often already exist in the household chest); it is clean, a wash under the tap after work making one's hands spotless; it can be either light or heavy work, whichever appeals to one; and it is invariably an economy, for one can make things that would often be costly to buy.

Before one can get the best out of a hobby, however, a certain fundamental knowledge is necessary, and the purpose of this book is to supply this knowledge and to provide suggestions and practical designs for things to make. The opening chapters deal with the choice, care and use of tools. These are followed by details of the various joints used in woodwork, how they are cut and when used. Finally there is a wide range of things to make, these being divided up under the headings of outdoor woodwork, small things to make and furniture. It will be seen that in nearly every case a cutting list is provided to assist in ordering materials. The usual allowance of about 10 mm in length and 3 mm to 6 mm in width is made. Thicknesses are net.

Nowadays, nearly all timber is sold in metric sizes, and we have therefore given dimensions and cutting lists in centimetres and millimetres. Many men, however, still use an Imperial rule, and we have therefore given on pages x and xi a conversion chart for those who prefer to work in inches and feet. The only point to watch is that it is desirable to work entirely in one or other of the standards. Otherwise, if, say, the overall length of a part is taken in inches, any subdivision may not work out exactly in millimetres.

Tools, too, are stamped in metric sizes to the nearest equivalent in inches, though, in fact, it makes little or no difference to their use. The *exact* length of a saw or plane does not affect its performance. The lengths of screws and nails also are not affected, though they may be sold in tens or hundreds rather than in dozens or grosses. The same applies to many fittings.

Metric Measurements and Conversion Tables

Timber is now converted to metric sizes but old stocks may still be available. However, the new sizes are only slightly smaller than the old Imperial sizes. Dimensions are based on 25 mm = 1 in. It is, in fact, a trifle less, but it makes little difference, providing one works to one or the other system throughout. We have given all metric sizes in the designs in these pages. It should be realised in buying timber from a yard that it is invariably sold in 'nominal' sizes. It will in fact finish less than this when planed. Thus a piece of 25-mm (1-in) softwood will finish no more than 22 mm ($\frac{7}{8}$ in).

The following are the sawn thicknesses in millimetres in which hardwood is converted: 19, 25, 32, 38, 50, 63, 75, 100, 125. Other thicknesses will have to be converted from one of the above, with corresponding loss in sawdust, or the next greater thickness will have to be planed down.

Softwood sawn thicknesses in millimetres are: 16, 19, 22, 25, 32, 38, 44, 50, 63, 75, 100, 150.

Plywood, blockboard and particle board are sold in millimetre thicknesses of: 3·2, 5·0, 6·5, 8·0, 9·5, 12·5, 16·0, 19·0, 22·0, 25·5, 32·0, 35·0, 38·0, 41·5, 44·5, 47·5.

It should be pointed out that the woodworker seldom goes into fine fractions or more than one decimal point. Just as in Imperial measurements he spoke of, say, $\frac{5}{16}$ in, $\frac{5}{16}$ in full, $5\frac{1}{2}$ sixteenths, $\frac{3}{8}$ in bare and $\frac{3}{8}$ in, giving a range of five measurements varying no more than $\frac{1}{16}$ in, he now applies the same idea to metric measurements, speaking of a millimetre full, bare or half.

Woodworkers' Conversion Tables

Imperial inches	Metric millimetres	Woodworkers' parlance
$\frac{1}{32}$	0·8	1 mm bare
$\frac{1}{16}$	1·6	$1\frac{1}{2}$ mm
$\frac{1}{8}$	3·2	3 mm full
$\frac{3}{16}$	4·8	5 mm bare
$\frac{1}{4}$	6·4	$6\frac{1}{2}$ mm
$\frac{5}{16}$	7·9	8 mm bare
$\frac{3}{8}$	9·5	$9\frac{1}{2}$ mm
$\frac{7}{16}$	11·1	11 mm full
$\frac{1}{2}$	12·7	$12\frac{1}{2}$ mm full
$\frac{9}{16}$	14·3	$14\frac{1}{2}$ mm bare
$\frac{5}{8}$	15·9	16 mm bare
$\frac{11}{16}$	17·5	$17\frac{1}{2}$ mm
$\frac{3}{4}$	19·1	19 mm full
$\frac{13}{16}$	20·6	$20\frac{1}{2}$ mm
$\frac{7}{8}$	22·2	22 mm full
$\frac{15}{16}$	23·8	24 mm bare
1	25·4	$25\frac{1}{2}$ mm
2	50·8	51 mm bare
3	76·2	76 mm full
4	101·4	$101\frac{1}{2}$ mm
5	127·0	127 mm
6	152·4	$152\frac{1}{2}$ mm
7	177·5	178 mm bare
8	203·2	203 mm full
9	228·6	$228\frac{1}{2}$ mm
10	254·0	254 mm
11	279·5	$279\frac{1}{2}$ mm
12	304·8	305 mm bare
18	457·2	457 mm full
24	609·6	$609\frac{1}{2}$ mm
36	914·4	$914\frac{1}{2}$ mm

(In the trade dimensions are based on 1 in = 25 mm.)

Metric millimetres	Imperial inches	Woodworkers' parlance
1	0·039	$\frac{1}{16}$ in bare
2	0·078	$\frac{1}{16}$ in full
3	0·118	$\frac{1}{8}$ in bare
4	0·157	$\frac{5}{32}$ in
5	0·196	$\frac{3}{16}$ in full
6	0·236	$\frac{1}{4}$ in bare
7	0·275	$\frac{1}{4}$ in full
8	0·314	$\frac{5}{16}$ in
9	0·354	$\frac{3}{8}$ in bare
10	0·393	$\frac{3}{8}$ in full
20	0·787	$\frac{13}{16}$ in bare
30	1·181	$1\frac{3}{16}$ in
40	1·574	$1\frac{9}{16}$ in full
50	1·968	$1\frac{15}{16}$ in full
60	2·362	$2\frac{3}{8}$ in bare
70	2·755	$2\frac{3}{4}$ in
80	3·148	$3\frac{1}{8}$ in full
90	3·542	$3\frac{9}{16}$ in bare
100	3·936	$3\frac{15}{16}$ in
150	5·904	$5\frac{15}{16}$ in bare
200	7·872	$7\frac{7}{8}$ in
300	11·808	$11\frac{13}{16}$ in
400	15·744	$15\frac{3}{4}$ in
500	19·680	$19\frac{11}{16}$ in
600	23·616	$23\frac{5}{8}$ in bare
700	27·552	$27\frac{9}{16}$ in
800	31·488	$31\frac{1}{2}$ in
900	35·424	$35\frac{7}{16}$ in
1000	39·360	$39\frac{3}{8}$ in bare

Remember!

Cheap tools are never cheap.

Spending time in sharpening tools is saving time.

Keep your left hand behind the chisel edge—it can't cut backwards.

Don't force a saw. If it cuts too slowly have it sharpened.

You are more likely to cut yourself using a blunt chisel than a sharp one.

Don't blame the tools when the joint doesn't fit.

If a piece of wood has nails in it it is safer to borrow someone else's saw.

If you drop a chisel don't try to catch it.

Don't pile tools on top of a saw; it costs money to have the latter sharpened.

Stopping may be the woodworker's friend, but he is rather doubtful company in which to be seen.

Cold Scotch glue doesn't stick; it merely congeals.

Veneer may hide shoddy work, but only for a little while.

Don't sharpen your own saws. It is cheaper to pay a professional sharpener.

Keep your tools sharp, even if you do rough work only.

Borrowed tools are nearly always abused. Don't lend yours.

Don't use an oilstone dry; it costs too much to spoil.

The bad workman blames his tools; the good one keeps his sharp.

A job can't be true if the wood is not planed up square.

1 Tools: Their Use and Care

1.1 The Preliminary Kit and Tool Cupboard

A big kit of tools is not essential for simple woodwork, but there are certain essentials without which it is unreasonable to expect to do much work. We therefore give a list of tools which we advise the reader to have. For purely rough carpentry some of them might be omitted, whilst for better work some additional ones are needed. Extra tools can be purchased as occasion arises.

It is a mistake to buy so-called cheap tools because they really are not cheap in the long run. This does not mean that the finest precision tools are needed; what it does mean is that, if the price has been cut beyond certain limits, something has had to suffer, and faults do not take long to develop in tools. It is better to pay the price listed by any reputable tool-maker in his catalogue.

1.1.1 *Preliminary Kit of Tools*

In some cases it is an advantage to vary the tools somewhat. For instance, for garden carpentry a rather larger size of handsaw is desirable, whilst for toy-making a fretsaw or scrollsaw is certainly desirable. All these are matters that readers can best decide for themselves.

With regard to a bench, many a fine piece of work has been turned out on a kitchen table, but this is at best only a makeshift. Light benches can normally be obtained, but probably the reader will prefer to make his own. The framework of this should be as heavy as possible to avoid racking.

1.1.2 *Tool Cupboard*

It is advisable to have a tool cupboard in the workshop, not only to provide a place for everything but also to

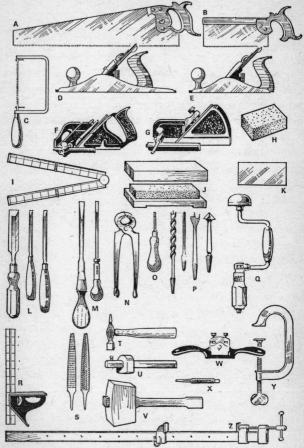

Fig. 1.1 Suggested preliminary kit of tools

The beginner is advised to invest in this kit at the outset.

A	Hand saw, cross-cut, 50 cm or 56 cm, fine teeth
B	Back saw, 23 cm or 25 cm, fine teeth
C	Coping saw
D	Adjustable metal jack plane, 50 mm cutter
E	„ „ smoothing plane, 50 mm cutter
F	„ „ rebate plane, 37 mm cutter
G	Grooving plane
H	Cork rubber
I	Rule, metric—Imperial
J	Oilstone, 20 cm by 50 mm
K	Scraper, 125 mm
L	Chisel, 19 mm bevel-edge
	„ 6 mm firmer
	„ 8 mm sash mortise
M	Screwdrivers, 150 mm cabinet type
	„ „ small ratchet
N	Pincers, 150 mm
O	Bradawl
P	Bit, 9·5 mm twist
	„ 3 mm shell or drill
	„ 19 mm centre
	„ snail countersink
Q	Brace, rachet, 20 cm sweep
R	Square, 30 cm metal adjustable
S	Rasp, 23 cm half-round
	File, 23 cm „ „
	A shaper also useful
T	Hammer, 227 g (8 oz) Warrington
U	Cutting gauge
V	Mallet, about 450 g (18 oz)
W	Spokeshave, metal or wood
X	Nail punch
Y	G cramp, about 15 cm
Z	Sash cramp, pair, 90 cm–120 cm

Details of the tools shown on page 16

enable tools to be locked away when not in use. The cupboard shown in Fig. 1.2 is of handy size for the small workshop and is large enough to hold a fair kit of tools. The sizes should be checked over with the actual tools, however, before a start is made. It may be that the saw or some other tool is extra large and may require an increase in height or width. The larger tools, such as planes, etc., are placed on the shelves behind the doors, and the last named are fitted with racks and clips to hold saws, chisels, screwdrivers and so on. In this connection, note that the shelves must stand in from the front sufficiently to enable the tools to clear. The top drawers can

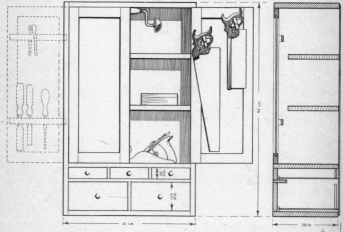

Fig. 1.2 Useful cupboard fitted for tools

be fitted with divisions to hold nails, screws and small fittings, whilst the larger lower drawers can take the smaller tools which would not hang conveniently behind the doors.

Since the cupboard is intended for the workshop, it can be made of deal and finished with paint or varnish. Fig. 1.3 shows a simple construction. The top and bottom ends of the sides are rebated to a depth equal to the thickness of the top and bottom. The rebates are cut easily by marking with the gauge, sawing *across* the grain and chopping out the waste *with* the grain. To hold the drawer divisions grooves are cut across. Here again, the saw is used to cut across the grain. The chisel removes the waste, and, if a router is available, this is used to make the groove of equal depth throughout.

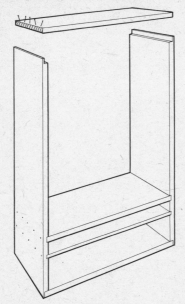

Fig. 1.3 Construction of tool cupboard

When cutting the top, bottom and drawer divisions to length, allowance must be made for the joints. For instance, the length of the top equals the overall width less the thickness of the two laps at the rebates. The whole thing is put together with glue and nails, and the last-named are dovetailed, that is driven in at an angle in alternate directions. The nails should be punched in and the holes filled in with plastic wood. Test for squareness, and nail a sheet of plywood on the back.

The doors are put together with mortise and tenon joints, the plywood panels preferably fitting in grooves. The chapter on door-making describes the procedure and gives alternative methods of construction. The tool racks are simply lengths of wood screwed to the inside with

Cutting List

	Long		Wide		Thick
	cm	mm	cm	mm	mm
2 Sides	95		31		25
Top, bottom, division					
3 Pieces	61		31		25
1 Division	61		7		12
2 Shelves	58		24		25
2 Uprights	—	75	7		12
1 Upright	15		7		12
1 Back	94		61		5 ply
4 Stiles	71		6		25
4 Rails	28		6		25
2 Panels	62		22		5 ply
3 Fronts	19		—	55	25
6 Sides	31		—	55	10
3 Backs	31		—	55	10
3 Bottoms	18		28		5 ply
2 Fronts	28		13		25
4 Sides	31		13		10
2 Backs	28		13		10
2 Bottoms	28		28		5 ply

Small parts are extra

little blocks between to bring them well clear of the doors, so allowing plenty of room for the tools. For the saws, shaped pieces to fit in the handles are screwed on (they can be screwed through the plywood from the front) and turn-buttons of wood screwed to these. Fig. 1.2 shows the idea. The shelves rest on fillets screwed to the cupboard sides.

The drawers can be either dovetailed or put together with lapped joints. For the method of making them, see Chapter 3, § 3.2.

1.2 Various Kinds of Saws

1.2.1 *The Hand Saw*

The hand saw is used for cutting up larger pieces of wood, and for general work a length of 50 cm or 56 cm is recommended. If only heavy carpentry is intended, a still larger saw could be chosen, but this is rather cumbersome for cabinet work. It should have fairly fine teeth and be a cross-cut, so that it can be used for both cross-cutting and ripping.

The tooth size is reckoned at so many to the inch, this being the actual number of points in an inch, including those at both ends. Today the word 'inch' is omitted. Ten points is a good all-round size.

When first obtained, it will be ready for immediate use, and a feature to note is that not only are the teeth sharp so far as the points are concerned but also it has 'set', which means that the teeth are bent over slightly in alternate directions. The reason for this is that the saw thus clears itself in the cut or kerf it makes, since the latter is wider than the thickness of the blade. If there were no set, the saw would bind in the kerf after the first few cuts and would be difficult to use.

Nails in the wood should be avoided at all costs. A single jar on a nail is enough to take off the edge—in bad cases it may break a tooth off. Do not attempt to sharpen it yourself unless you have had experience. It is seldom an economy because, if the teeth become uneven through faulty filing, a professional sharpener will charge more to put it right. Better by far to take it to a reliable sharpener as soon as it becomes dull.

A saw should never be forced. Keep it moving steadily
for nearly its full length. Its own weight plus the slightest
pressure is all that is needed. To start the cut place the
thumb of the left hand against the blade, as in Fig. 1.4.

Fig. 1.4 Cross-cutting with the
hand saw

Note how the thumb of
the left hand steadies the
blade at the start of the
cut.

Fig. 1.5 Coss-cutting—
completion of the
cut, left hand sup-
porting the over-
hang.

This steadies the blade, enabling it to start in the right
place, and prevents an accident in the event of the saw
jumping. Make one or two short movements, taking care
that the saw works in the right direction, and then give
full, easy strokes. When the end is reached, the left hand

can hold the overhanging piece, as in Fig. 1.5, to prevent it from breaking off and so splitting. Note that the index finger of the right hand points along the handle. This gives positive control.

A point to note in all sawing is that, as a rule, the cut is made to one side of the line. The latter represents the finished size of the wood, and if the saw were taken directly along it the wood would be too small. The cut is therefore made on the waste side, as shown in Fig. 1.6, so that the wood can afterwards be trimmed with the plane.

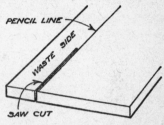

Fig. 1.6 Sawing to pencil line

1.2.2 *The Back Saw*
When one saw only is being used, a length of 23 cm or 25 cm is useful, though the ideal is to have a 36-cm tenon saw for heavy cutting and a 20-cm dovetail saw for fine joints.

The cut is made on the waste side.

Fig. 1.7 shows the saw in use, and it will be seen that the wood is held on what is known as a bench hook. This steadies the wood, and it is easily made from odd scraps, as shown in Fig. 1.8. One point to note is that the strip that bears against the edge of the bench should be fixed on with dowels rather than with nails or screws. It is inevitable that, with continuous use, the wood will gradually be sawn away, and this may result in the nails becoming bared, so jarring the saw.

For the tenon saw, choose one with about twelve or fourteen points. If, however, only the one 25-cm saw is being bought, it should have teeth not larger than fourteen points. A dovetail saw could have sixteen points.

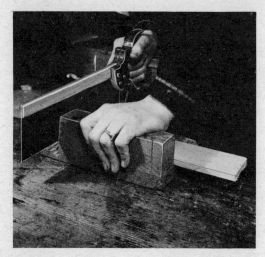

Fig. 1.7 Wood being held on the bench hook whilst being sawn

The purpose of this is to steady the wood. Note how the left-hand thumb bears against the blade of the saw.

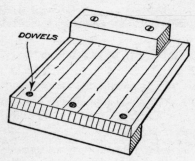

DOWELS

Fig. 1.8 Details of the bench hook

1.2.3 *Saws for Cutting Shapes*

The serious woodworker will need saws for cutting shapes. The bow saw is the most useful, since the blade is under constant tension. It is shown in use in Fig. 1.9. It is gripped with both hands, the wood being held steady in the vice. The handles to which the blade is attached are

Fig. 1.9 How the bow saw is used

Note that the blade is turned to enable it to cut horizontally.

free to turn, so that the saw can be used to cut in a direction parallel to the edge. Otherwise, its use would be limited by the depth of the blade from the cross-bar. When cutting interior holes, the rivet is knocked out at one handle, thus freeing the blade. The latter can then be passed through a hole drilled in the wood and the rivet replaced.

There is, of course, a limit to the distance from the edge at which this saw can cut, and when its use is impracticable the keyhole saw is needed. This is shown in Fig. 1.10. Note that the blade can be made to slide into the handle, and the general rule is to have out only as much blade as is necessary for the work because the saw buckles so easily.

Fig. 1.10 Sides of keyhole being cut with the keyhole saw

Another handy tool is the coping saw. Thin wood and small work can be cut satisfactorily with this. It is shown at *C*, Fig. 1.1, page 16.

1.3 Use of the Plane

1.3.1 *The Jack Plane*
This is the 'maid-of-all-work' plane. It can be set coarse, so enabling the thickness of a piece of wood to be reduced quickly, and its length prevents it from digging in and producing an uneven surface. The professional wood-

worker generally reserves it for the rougher sort of work, since he has a long trying plane with which to shoot joints and true-up a surface. Today many men use the adjustable metal plane. Its sharpening and setting are as for the wood plane, but there is no wedge, the cutter being held by a lever clamp. The hammer is never used.

1.3.2 *The Cutting Action*

It is desirable to understand how a plane works if one is to turn out good work. First of all there is the question of its length. A smoothing plane is liable to dig into the wood, producing a curve which runs through points located at the front and back of the plane and through the edge of the cutter. It is obvious that the farther apart the front and back, the less the plane can dig in. Hence the necessity for a long plane when long surfaces are to be trued up.

The back-iron plays an important part. Its purpose is to break the shaving, so robbing it of its strength and thus largely preventing it from splitting out. If there were no back-iron, the actual edge of the cutter would not be making the cut because the shaving would be levered up, with the result that it would be torn up, so leaving corresponding tears on the surface of the wood. By fitting a back-iron, the shaving is broken almost as soon as it is raised and is not so liable to tear out. The closer the back-iron is to the edge, the less liable it is to tear out the wood; but, on the other hand, the resistance is increased considerably. For normal work, a compromise is effected, fitting the back-iron about $1\frac{1}{2}$ mm from the edge. When a piece of wood with difficult grain has to be planed, the back-iron is advanced and the plane set as fine as possible.

The mouth, too, has to be considered. When small, it stops the shaving from being raised too soon and thus helps to prevent tearing out. There is a limit to the size, however, since too fine a mouth may cause choking.

1.3.3 *Sharpening the Plane*

To sharpen the plane remove the cutter by undoing the lever cap of the metal plane or striking the button of a wood plane and undo the screw holding the back-iron. The latter can then be slid off. Put a few drops of oil on

Fig. 1.11 Sharpening the plane-iron

The correct angle is in the region of 30 degrees.

the stone and place the cutter on the latter so that the ground bevel lies flat. Now, raise the hands *slightly* so that just the edge of the cutter is touching the stone, and work back and forth, as shown in Fig. 1.11. This will turn up a burr at the back which can be detected by drawing the thumb *across* the edge at the back. This is an indication that it is sharp, and the burr is turned back by reversing the cutter *flat* on the stone and moving back and forth once or twice, as shown in Fig. 1.12. It is then stropped either on a piece of leather glued to a flat board or by drawing it *across* the left hand, first one side and then the other (Fig. 1.13). It should be noted that it is of the utmost importance that the back is not dubbed over either on the stone or on the leather strop.

Fig. 1.12 Turning back burr from the plane-iron

It is essential that the iron is kept flat.

Drawing the thumb across the edge is an indication whether or not it is sharp, but it does not show whether a gash, such as might be caused by a nail, is taken out. This is best ascertained by holding the cutter to the light. A sharp edge cannot be seen, whereas a dull one will show as a thin line of light. Similarly, any gashes will show up light. It is then a case of rubbing down until the whole edge is sharp.

The cutting edge of a jack-plane iron should be slightly rounded so that, when used on a board, the shavings taper away to nothing at the sides. The roundness must not be overdone, as this will cause bad hollows in the surface. In fact, when required for close trueing-up, it should be almost straight, with just the corners taken off to prevent them from digging in.

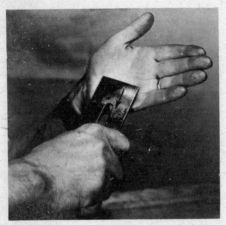

Fig. 1.13 Stropping the cutter

> It is drawn *across* the hand, first one side and then the other.

The back-iron is now replaced, and the two are put in the plane and held by the thumb of the left hand. By placing the plane over a sheet of paper and holding it in line with the eye, as in Fig. 1.14, the projection of the cutter can be seen. It should appear as a thin black line. The wedge of the wood plane can then be knocked in. More projection can be given by tapping the back of the cutter, less by tapping the striking button lightly.

Fig. 1.15 shows how the plane is used on broad surfaces. The left hand grasps the knob. The important parts
are the beginning and ending of the stroke. Dubbing over

Fig. 1.14 Sighting the smoothing plane when setting

> The white paper on the bench shows up the line of
> the cutter.

must be avoided at all costs. At the start, exert plenty of
downward pressure at the front and, as the far end is
reached, change over the pressure to the back. This is
shown clearly in Fig. 1.16.

The left hand should be held as shown in Fig. 1.17 when planing an edge, the fingers touching the side of the wood and so acting as a sort of gauge or fence. The

Fig. 1.15 Using the plane on a broad surface

The left hand bears down on top of the plane.

simplest way of shooting an edge straight is to set the plane fine and remove as much wood as possible from the centre until the plane will cut no more. One or two shavings along the whole length will then produce a straight edge, providing the plane is true and the wood

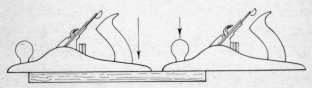

Fig. 1.16 Where pressure is applied when planing

not too long. For a start, however, it is advisable to test with a straight-edge—also with a square to see that it is at right angles with the sides.

To prevent the grain from splitting out when planing end grain the far corner can be chiselled off as at *B*, Fig.

Fig. 1.17 Holding the plane when planing an edge

Note how the fingers of left hand pass under the sole and bear against the wood to act as a sort of fence.

1.18, or by temporarily cramping on a block of wood as at *C*. The block supports the corner.

A shooting board is an invaluable appliance, both for planing the edges of thin wood and for trimming the ends square. It is easily made, as shown in Fig. 1.19. The length can be fixed in accordance with the usual size of

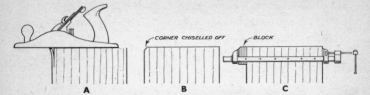

Fig. 1.18 Points to note when planing end grain

    A   How far corner is liable to split out
    B, C Methods of avoiding the splitting

work to be done. It is shown in use in Fig. 1.20. When two boards are to be jointed, a face-mark is made on each. They are then planed, one with the face side uppermost and the other with the face side downwards. The reason for this is that, if the plane works a trifle out of square, the reversing of the second board gives it a precisely

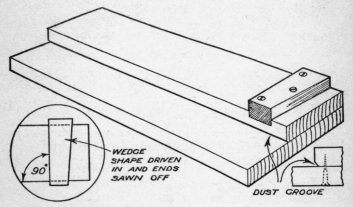

Fig. 1.19 Simple shooting board

    The lower corner of the top piece is slightly bevelled to form a groove for dust.

opposite angle and the two go together in perfect alignment.

1.3.4 *The Smoothing Plane*

The metal type of smoothing plane is recommended rather than the wood plane. It is so handy for fine work on the shooting board and in all work generally. One

Fig. 1.20 Planing thin wood on shooting board

> This ensures the edge being square, since the plane cannot wobble.

point to note is that all metal planes require lubricating. A piece of candle rubbed on the sole occasionally or a wad of cotton wool soaked in linseed oil can be used. As the plane is used for final cleaning up on wide surfaces, the cutter edge should be almost straight, with the corners taken off.

1.3.5 *The Rebate Plane*

For some jobs this is essential. It is shown in use in Fig. 1.21. Metal rebate planes are available, and these possess the advantage of having a fence which enables the rebate to be automatically kept parallel with the edge. There is also an adjustable depth stop, the plane ceasing to cut when the required depth is reached.

For grooves, the small grooving plane (as shown at *G*, Fig. 1.1) is invaluable.

Fig. 1.21 The rebate plane in use

The spur of the plane is used only when working across the grain.

1.4 The Scraper

The scraper is used entirely for cleaning up. A plane, no matter how finely set, is bound to leave a number of 'waves', due to the shape of the cutter, and the scraper is used to take out these. Furthermore, some woods have difficult grain, which is liable to tear out even when the back-iron is set close, and the scraper, taking an ex-

tremely fine shaving, can be used to take out tears left by
the plane. Then, again, for cleaning up veneered surfaces
the scraper is essential, since the plane would take too
coarse a shaving.

A scraper should be of medium thickness. If too thick,
it will require a great deal of exertion to keep bent (a
scraper is bent slightly in use by the thumbs, as shown in
Fig. 1.22), which will prove tiring. On the other hand, a

Fig. 1.22 How scraper is used to clean up panel

> It is held obliquely when working over a cross-
> banding to reduce risk of tearing out the grain.

thin scraper will rapidly become hot and burn the
thumbs. Somewhere in the region of a full millimetre is
about right.

The cutting edge is obtained by turning up a burr as at
F, Fig. 1.23, and to enable this to be done the edges must
first be made square and smooth. Fixing the scraper in
the vice, rub down each long edge with a flat file, as
shown at *A*. This will make it true, but the file-marks must
be got rid of by rubbing on the stone (*B*). If it is worked on

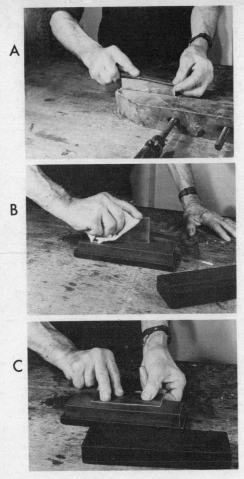

Fig. 1.23 Stages in sharpening the scraper

       A Filing the edge
       B Rubbing edge on the oilstone
       C Flattening side on the oilstone

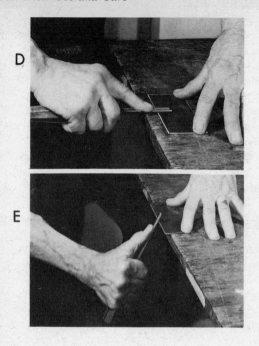

D Rubbing down the side with the gouge or ticketer
E Turning the edge with the gouge or ticketer
F Diagram showing how scraper works

the edge of the stone with the cover opened slightly, there will be a good guide for holding it upright. It should be grasped with a piece of rag to prevent an accident. To get rid of the inevitable ragged burr the sides are now rubbed down as shown at *C*, the scraper being held perfectly flat on the stone. Afterwards, a few rubs can again be given on the edge.

The actual cutting burr is now turned up by using a hard steel instrument such as a gouge. The scraper should be placed on the bench with the edge overhanging about 6 mm and a sharp stroke made with the gouge first in one direction, then in the other, as shown at *E*, the gouge being held a few degrees out of the vertical. If the thumb is drawn *across* the edge, the turned-up burr will be apparent. All four edges are treated in the same way.

After being in use for a time, the edges will lose their keenness and will require to be turned again. To do this the scraper is held flat and the gouge drawn along each side in turn, as shown at *D*, the blade being held perfectly flat. The turning process is then repeated as at *E*. This rubbing down and turning with the gouge can be done several times until it fails to produce a keen edge, after which the scraper must be again rubbed down with file and stone.

Normally, the scraper can be held at right angles with the grain, but if the grain is specially difficult, or if there is a cross-banding or inlay, it is advisable to hold it at an angle, as shown in Fig. 1.22.

1.5 The Spokeshave and Rasp

1.5.1 *The Spokeshave*

The spokeshave is used for shaped surfaces. Two kinds are available, those of wood and those of metal, and each can be obtained with either a flat face (used mainly for convex shapes) or a round face (for cleaning up concave surfaces).

Fig. 1.24 shows the wooden type in use. The important point to watch is the direction of the grain, because the

Fig. 1.24 The wood spokeshave in use

The tool should always be worked *into* the grain.

tool is liable to cause the grain to tear out badly if worked against it. Fig. 1.25 shows the idea. To sharpen the cutter either a stone slip may be used or the usual oilstone must be turned on edge, as in Fig. 1.26. The cutter is ground hollow, and it should be held flat on the stone, as at *A*. It is not necessary to turn back the burr after sharpening.

Fig. 1.25 Use of spokeshave

How grain affects direction in which spokeshave is worked.

Cutters of the metal spokeshave are sharpened like an ordinary plane-iron, but a holder such as that shown in Fig. 1.27 should be made.

1.5.2 *Rasps and Files*

These are useful for cleaning up some curved surfaces. For instance, certain concave shapes are so quick that the

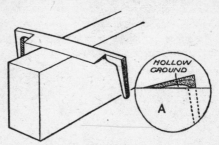

Fig. 1.26 Sharpening spokeshave cutter

spokeshave cannot enter them, and here a file is invaluable. Scratches left by the file can be taken out with the scraper and glasspaper. Examples are given in Fig. 1.28.

1.6 Shaper Tools

Modern forms of shaper tools are used for similar purposes to files and have the advantage of being free from all liability to choke. They are specially handy for substances that are awkward to plane or chisel—chipboard, for example.

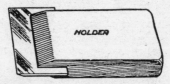

Fig. 1.27 Holder for metal spokeshave cutter

1.7 Chisels

The firmer chisel is the most useful for general purposes. It is sturdily built so that it will stand up to heavy use, such as chopping out, when it has to be struck with the mallet, and it can be used for paring, though the more delicate bevelled-edge chisel is more convenient for the latter operation. Both are shown in Fig. 1.29.

The firmer chisel is sharpened similarly to the plane-iron, though, being narrow, it should not be worked continuously in the middle of the stone as this will rapidly cause the latter to become hollow. Hold it with the bevel flat on the stone and then raise the handle a trifle so that a new bevel is formed. The correct angle is from 30 to 35 degrees. Do not raise the handle unduly as this will create a thick edge, with the result that it will lose much of its keenness. In practice, it will be found that the bevelled-edge type can have a lower angle, because the chisel is used only for paring work. For the firmer type, a rather more substantial edge is needed, owing to the heavier type of work for which it is required. The sharpening is shown in Fig. 1.30. When a burr has been turned up, the chisel is reversed and rubbed once or twice *flat* on the stone.

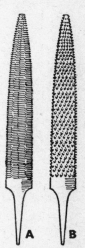

Fig. 1.28

A Wood file
B Wood rasp

1.7.1 *Using the Chisel*
Always hold the left hand *behind* the cutting edge when chiselling. If this is done, an accident is practically impos-

sible. Two paring operations are shown in Figs. 1.31 and 1.32. In the former a groove is being cleaned up. A sideways movement should be given as well as a forward one, so that the tool makes a slicing cut. Some prefer to hold the thumb of the left hand above the chisel. It is a matter of personal preference.

In Fig. 1.32 a corner is being taken off. Note that the wood rests upon a flat, solid part of the bench so that it does not splinter out the underside. The finger of the left hand passing round the chisel both guides and steadies the blade.

The handle should be struck with the mallet when chopping out has to be done. A hammer will soon fray out the end. The firmer chisel only is used. One branch of chopping out is in cutting a mortise, and, though the firmer can be used, there is a danger that it may snap. Consequently, a special form of chisel made for the purpose is used. An example is shown at *C* in Fig. 1.29. It is known as a sash chisel and is not quite so cumbersome as the full mortise type. The method of chopping a mortise is dealt with in a later section, but it may be mentioned here that the most useful size is 8 mm. The reason for this is that most wood to be mortised is 23 mm thick, and, as the mortise should be as near one-third of

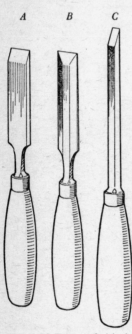

A   B   C

Fig. 1.29 Types of chisels

A Firmer
B Bevelled-edge
C Sash

Fig. 1.30 How chisel is held when sharpening

It is afterwards reversed *flat* on the stone to turn back the burr.

Fig. 1.31 Paring groove with bevelled-edge chisel

The thumb of the left hand steadies the blade.

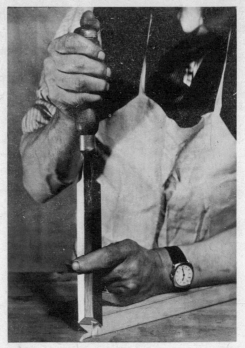

Fig. 1.32 Paring corner with chisel

> Note how index finger of left hand passes round
> blade to steady it.

the thickness as possible, this size most nearly fulfils that
requirement.

1.8 Various Tools

1.8.1 *Tools for Boring*
For most work, a brace with a 20-cm sweep is the most
useful. Those who care to go to the extra expense might
with advantage obtain a ratchet brace, because this is so

handy when working in a corner. A brace of this kind is shown in Fig. 1.1. It is important that it be held upright, and a good plan for a start is to place a square on the bench at the side as a guide, as shown in Fig. 1.33. One point to note is that it is easier to tell whether a brace

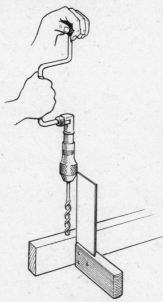

Fig. 1.33 Use of square when boring

leans to the left or right than whether it is leaning away from or towards one. Consequently, for such jobs as dowelling, where it would be fatal for the bit to run out at the side, the worker should stand at the end. Should the hole lean a trifle along the length of the work it would not be so disastrous, though it would obviously be better for it to be perfectly upright.

One of the most useful bits is the 9·5-mm twist-bit,

because it is needed in dowelling. A smaller one, 6 mm, is handy when mortising to clear out the bulk of the waste before chopping. When a number of holes have to be bored to the same depth, either a piece of paper can be stuck to the bit as a guide (Fig. 1.34) or a depth gauge can be fixed on (Fig. 1.35). The latter is easily made from two pieces of wood screwed together with a centre notch to hold the bit.

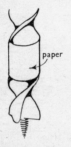
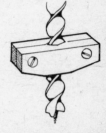

Fig. 1.34 Paper stuck to bit to   **Fig. 1.35** Depth gauge fixed
act as depth gauge   to bit

Centre-bits are suitable only for boring comparatively shallow holes. For deep holes in end grain they are useless, because they are liable to drift with the grain since there is no spiral portion, as in a twist-bit, to keep them true.

A drill-bit is handy for boring screw-holes. A size of about 3 mm is the most useful. A countersink is also needed. This seldom requires sharpening, but a few rubs with a small, flat file and a rat-tail file soon restore its edge.

Another invaluable tool for use in screwing is the bradawl. In use, the blade should point across the grain. To sharpen it the oilstone can be used, or if gashed it can first be rubbed down with a file.

1.8.2 *The Oilstone*

An oilstone is an essential part of the kit. To prevent it from shifting about a piece of leather can be glued underneath at each end. Do not try to economise unduly on the stone. A cheap one is generally useless—or rapidly becomes so. An 'Indian' or a 'Carborundum' stone is excellent. 'Washita' stones, too, are good, though one occasionally comes across one that becomes hard and loses its cut. Use a good-quality, fairly thin oil and wipe the stone after use. A slip is needed for sharpening some gouges and is also handy for the spokeshave.

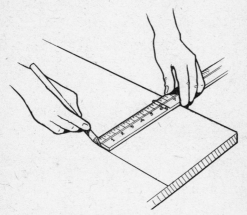

Fig. 1.36 Marking line parallel with edge

1.8.3 *Marking and Testing Tools*

A metric-Imperial rule is convenient for general use. When marking a size, it should be turned on edge so that the calibrations actually touch the wood. Long lengths of timber can be marked out parallel from one straight edge by using the index finger of the left hand as a gauge (Fig. 1.36), though such marking is only approximate.

A square is needed for both marking and testing, and a point to note about its use is that the butt should always bear against either the face side or the face edge. A similar tool to the square is the set-mitre, used for testing mitres. The blade is set at 45 degrees.

A gauge is essential for accurate work. Two kinds are available, the marking and the cutting gauge. The latter is

Fig. 1.37 Use of the cutting gauge

> This can be used across the grain, as here, as well as *with* it.

recommended because it can be used *across* the grain as well as with it. Fig. 1.37 shows how it is held. When working *with* the grain, be careful to avoid allowing the gauge to run with the grain. The inward pressure of the second finger helps to prevent this.

When mortising, a mortise gauge is needed. This is a similar tool but is provided with a second adjustable marker, as shown in Fig. 1.38.

1.8.4 *Other Tools*

The hammer is a fairly obvious requirement. The Warrington pattern with flat pane is recommended. A punch is also useful for sinking nails. A medium size of screwdriver is best to begin with. Pincers are needed when nailing, and a useful tip here is that, to avoid bruising the wood, a piece of flat steel such as a scraper can be placed underneath, as shown in Fig. 1.39. A

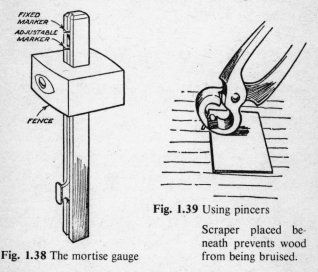

Fig. 1.38 The mortise gauge

Fig. 1.39 Using pincers

Scraper placed beneath prevents wood from being bruised.

mallet is required for striking chisels, as this will not fray the handles. The cork rubber is required when glasspapering because, if the glasspaper is held in the hand only, it will not take out any inequalities and the corners are liable to be dubbed over. Fig. 1.40 shows how it should (and should not) be used.

Cramps are needed when glueing up, and to hold down wood while being worked. A couple of sash cramps (*Z*, Fig. 1.1) are invaluable when assembling doors, glued

joints and so on. Thumbscrews are handy for small work
and handscrews or G cramps for larger pieces.

For mitreing mouldings, the mitre block for small

Fig. 1.40 Use of cork rubber

A Correct use. Note where pressure is applied
B Faulty use, showing ends dubbed over

work and the mitre box for large work are really essential. They are shown in Fig. 1.41. This illustration also
shows a mitre shooting board used for trimming mitres
after sawing.

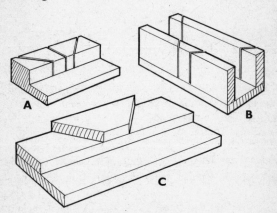

Fig. 1.41 Appliances for mitreing

A Mitre block
B Mitre box
C Mitre shooting board

Fig. 1.42 Basic power unit with circular saw and planes, available also as a basic lathe

1.9 Drills

Electric drills are widely used in the workshop, especially in conjunction with the various attachments made for them. These include the circular saw, disc sander, orbital sander, lathe, moulder and so on.

2 Joints and Their Application

2.1 Nailed and Screwed Joints

2.1.1 *Nailing*

Although nailing seems an obvious sort of thing, there are right and wrong ways of doing it, and there are undoubtedly pitfalls. For instance, there is the old danger of splitting when nails are driven in at the end of a board. In such a case it is always a safeguard to bore the holes first.

A simple corner joint is shown in Fig. 2.1, and it will be noticed that the nails are staggered. This again helps in preventing the wood from splitting.

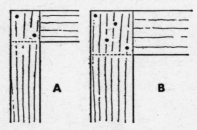

Fig. 2.1 Nailing framework corners

A Two-nail
B Four-nail

When a simple box is being made with nailed corners, it is important that the edges are square; otherwise, there will be a gap at one side—as at *A*, Fig. 2.2, which is weak, apart from being unsightly—or the parts will fit together out of square—as at *B*. The strength of such a joint can be increased by 'dovetailing' the nails—that is, driving them in askew in alternate directions. For rough

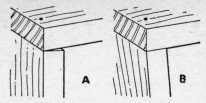

Fig. 2.2 Faults in nailing

> There is either a gap, as at *A*, or parts are out of square, as at *B*.

work, in which the parts are put together in their thickness, long nails can be used so that they can be clenched at the back.

2.1.2 *Screwing*

Screws are obtainable in various forms and metals, but the most commonly used are the countersunk, roundhead and raisedhead shown in Fig. 2.3. This illustration shows how the lengths of screws are calculated. In all cases the wood that holds the shank should be bored with an easy clearance fit. It should never be tight. It is only the wood into which the screw portion is driven that should be tight. The hole should be about the size of the diameter of the centre portion, so that the spiral flange or screw part bites into the wood and so holds. This is shown clearly in Fig. 2.4.

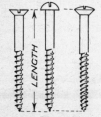

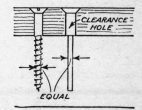

Fig. 2.3 How length of screws is calculated

Fig. 2.4 Sizes of holes bored when screwing

In the ordinary way there is no difficulty about countersinking a screw, but sometimes a thick piece of wood has to be screwed to a comparatively thin piece. For example, a tabletop is often screwed on, and to drive the screws right through the rails would necessitate long screws. The method known as pocket screwing is therefore usually adopted. This is shown in Fig. 2.5, in which a cut is made with a gouge in the inside of the rail,

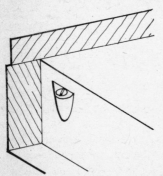

enabling a shorter screw to be used. To do this the clearance hole is bored at an angle from the top edge of the rail, so that it emerges inside. The gouge-cut is then made deep enough to take the head of the screw.

2.2. Glued Joints

Fig. 2.5 Method of pocket screwing

When it is required to produce a wide surface, it is necessary to glue together two or more pieces. In the best form the two parts are planed to make a perfect joint and are 'rubbed' together—that is, the one piece is fixed in the vice, the surfaces are glued, and the upper piece is placed in position and rubbed back and forth so that all surplus glue is squeezed out. The advantage of this is that the parts retain their natural shape. It is satisfactory for joints up to about 90 cm in length. For longer work, however, it is desirable to use cramps, and in this case the joint is shot a trifle hollow and one or more cramps are put on in the centre. In this way the ends are naturally pressed tightly together—a desirable feature because the ends are the most vulnerable points.

The first step is to mark the joining edges so that the parts can be replaced in the correct positions. The joints can be shot either in the vice or on the shooting board. In the former case a square should be used to test the edges to ensure that the two pieces are in alignment. When the shooting board is used, the one piece is planed with the face side uppermost and the other with the face side downwards. In this way they will fit together square.

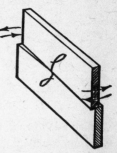

If the joint is held to the light, it can be seen whether it is making a close fit; but, in any case, the upper piece should be swivelled

Fig. 2.6 Testing joint by 'swivelling'

back and forth, as shown in Fig. 2.6. A round joint will merely pivot at the centre, whereas a correctly planed one will give friction at the ends, showing that they are touching.

In all cases when Scotch glue is used, the joints should be heated to prevent the glue from chilling, and, when rubbing the upper piece, the hands should be kept low at the ends so that the joint is not broken. This is shown in Fig. 2.7. When the glue is drying, the joints can be

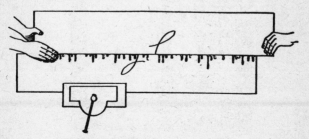

Fig. 2.7 How long joint is rubbed

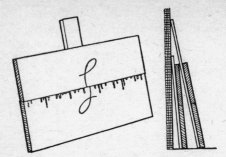

Fig. 2.8 Stacking joints whilst drying

stacked as shown in Fig. 2.8, each resting across its entire width on a batten.

It is advisable to test a cramped joint with the straight-edge, as shown in Fig. 2.9, because if the cramp is not put

Fig. 2.9 Testing cramped joint with straight-edge

on correctly it may tend to pull the joint out of alignment. If the upper piece leans forward, the cramp should be put farther back.

Thin wood of, say, 3 mm thickness should be planed on the shooting board, because otherwise it is difficult to keep the edge square. When glueing up, two battens are laid on the bench, a sheet of paper is placed over them and the joint rubbed together flat, as shown in Fig. 2.10. If cramps are required, as in the case of a long joint, battens must be put on with thumbscrews at both sides to prevent buckling.

PAPER UNDER JOINT

Fig. 2.10 Assembling joint in thin wood

2.3 Halved Joints

Fig. 2.11(i) shows a halved joint used for joining two pieces at right angles, the joint occurring at the centre. The width of the wood is marked across with chisel and square, as at A, and returned at the edges with pencil marks. To mark the depth the gauge is used from the face side in both cases, so that the two parts are bound to fit together level even if the gauge is not set exactly to the middle. The sides of the groove are cut in with the saw, and, to provide a channel in which the saw can run, a small sloping groove is made with the chisel on the waste side. After sawing the sides, the waste is chiselled first

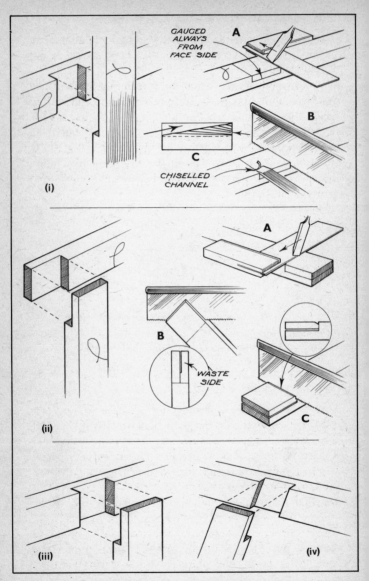

Fig. 2.11 Types of halved joints and how they are cut

When the waste is sawn away, the saw is held to the side of the line so that the latter is left in.

from one side (left at *C*) and then from the other, as
shown by the arrows.

The corner halved joint illustrated in Fig. 2.11(ii)
needs the use of the saw only for cutting. It is marked out
with chisel and square as at *A*, a small extra allowance
being made in the length for trimming. As before, the line
of the halving is gauged from the face side only, and when
being cut the saw is worked at the side of the line, as
shown inset at *B*. It is best to fix the wood in the vice at an
angle and cut down as far as the diagonal. It can then be
reversed—this time upright, and the cut completed. *C*
shows the shoulder being sawn.

Fig. 2.11(iii) is a combination of the two joints already
given, known as a T halving, and Fig. 2.11(iv) shows a
similar joint with the one member set obliquely.

2.4 Mortise and Tenon Joints

The mortise and tenon joint has many applications. Its
simplest form is shown at *A*, Fig. 2.12. The thickness of
the tenon is as near as possible one-third that of the wood.
It is used for simple doors, frames and all similar jobs in
which two comparatively narrow pieces are joined
together at right angles.

A rather more elaborate variation is that shown at *B*,
in which the wood is rebated at the back to hold a panel
as in a door. This means that the back shoulder has to be
cut longer than the front one by an amount equal to the
depth of the rebate. When making it, the rebate is marked
out with the gauge, but is not worked until after both
mortise and tenon have been cut.

C is similar to that shown at *A* but has a haunch at the
top to prevent any twisting tendency. As the haunch is
tapered, it is invisible at the top. The joint is used when
two rails have to be joined to a leg. Note from the inset

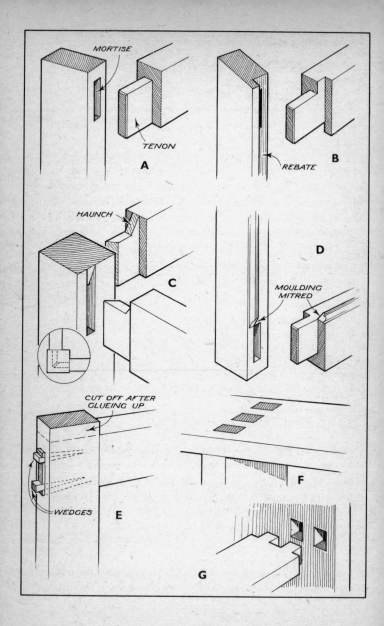

sketch how the ends of the tenons are cut at an angle so that they have the maximum length.

At *D* the wood is rebated, but a moulding is worked at the front edge. In this case, the shoulders are level because the moulding is cut away and mitred. It should be noted that, when a door is made, the shoulder length is taken from the rebate depth, not from the edge of the moulding.

A joint useful for outdoor work is the through-wedged type shown at *E*. The mortise is cut extra long at the outer edge and two saw-cuts are made, one at each side of the tenon. After glueing up, a wedge is driven into each so that it is impossible to pull the two apart.

2.4.1 *Making the Simple Mortise and Tenon Joint*
Fig. 2.13 shows the stages in cutting the mortise and tenon joints when making a door. Having planed up the wood, the two pieces for the rails are fixed together and the shoulder positions marked out, as at *B*. After marking both together as shown, they are separated and the marks squared around both individually on all four sides. The stiles follow as at *C*. A mortise gauge is now set so that the two markers are spaced to the width of chisel being used. The fence is set so that the two marks are central, and all the parts are marked from the face side, as shown at *D*.

Chopping the mortises is shown at *E* and *F*. A great

Fig. 2.12 Various forms of mortise and tenon joints

    A Simple mortise and tenon joint
    B Joint for rebated framework
    C Haunched tenons meeting at leg
    D Framework with mitred moulding worked in the solid
    E Through tenon wedged at outside
    F Through tenons for carcase work
    G Drawer rail joint

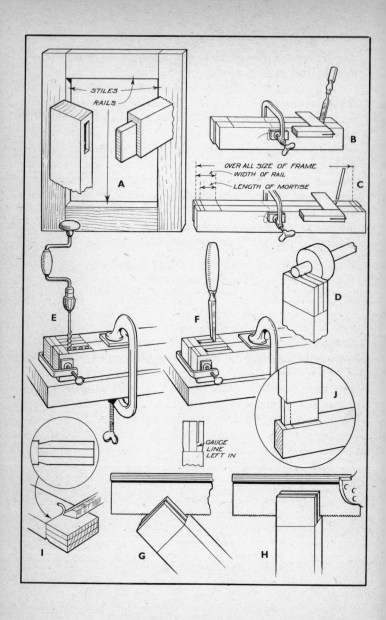

STILES

RAILS

A

B

OVER ALL SIZE OF FRAME
WIDTH OF RAIL
LENGTH OF MORTISE

C

E

F

D

GAUGE
LINE
LEFT IN

J

I

G

H

deal of the waste is removed by boring, using a bit slightly smaller than the mortise width. The chopping follows as at *F*. The chisel is started at the middle and is struck with the mallet. It is gradually worked first towards one end, then towards the other, the depth being increased at each cut.

When the tenons are sawn, the wood should be fixed in the vice at an angle and the cut taken down as far as the diagonal, as shown at *G*. It is then reversed, this time upright, and the cut completed as at *H*. Note that the cuts should be made *outside* the gauge lines so that the latter are just left in. Before sawing the shoulders, a chisel-cut should be made as at *I*. This forms a channel in which the saw can run.

The last job is fitting the tenons. Each tenon is placed opposite its mortise, as shown at *J*, and a pencil mark made. The waste is then sawn away and any final fitting completed.

2.5 Dovetail Joints

2.5.1 *Various Kinds of Dovetails*
The simplest form of dovetail is shown at *A* in Fig. 2.14. One of the commonest ways in which it is used is in

Fig. 2.13 Cutting mortise and tenon joints for a door

> *A* Door with joint in detail
> *B* Marking the rails
> *C* Marking the stiles
> *D* Using mortise gauge
> *E* Boring away the waste
> *F* Chopping the mortises
> *G* First stage in sawing tenons
> *H* Finishing tenons
> *I* Cutting channel at shoulder
> *J* Fitting the joint

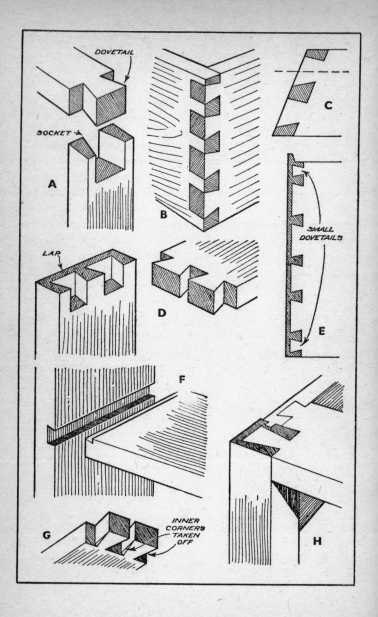

DOVETAIL

SOCKET

A

B

C

LAP

D

SMALL
DOVETAILS

E

F

G

INNER
CORNERS
TAKEN
OFF

H

joining the sides of a box (*B*). Simple cabinet carcases, frames of various kinds and drawers call for its use. Sometimes one of the joining pieces has to be at an angle, as at *C*, and here it should be noted that the slope of the dovetail is set out equally at the sides of a line parallel with the sides of the piece in which the dovetails are cut.

Lapped dovetails are used when the joint requires to be concealed at one side. An example is given at *D*. The only difference in the marking out is that the gauge giving the dovetail length is set to the thickness of the wood in which the sockets are cut, less the thickness of the lap.

A bare-faced housed dovetail is given at *F*. These joints are handy when fixed shelves have to be fitted to a tall bookcase. The joint is easier to fit if made tapered. The joint at *H* is a lap dovetail as applied to a table framework. The side rail is tenoned to the leg and is glued up. The front rail is then dovetailed in as shown.

2.5.2. *Cutting a Through Dovetail*

When dovetailing two pieces together, the ends to be jointed must be planed square. A cutting gauge is set to the thickness of the wood and both pieces are gauged all round, as shown in Fig. 2.15. The position of the dovetails is now marked in with pencil. A slope of 12 mm of 15 mm in 75 mm is correct (Fig. 2.16). Fig. 2.17 shows the dovetails being cut.

Fig. 2.14 Various forms of dovetails

    A Through dovetail
    B Through dovetails applied to a box
    C Correct slope when piece with sockets is at an angle
    D Lapped dovetail
    E Lapped dovetails for cabinet carcase top
    F Barefaced housed dovetail
    G Corners taken off to ease assembling
    H Lapped dovetails of table framework

Fig. 2.15 Gauging the ends

The gauge is set to the thickness of the wood.

To transfer these marks the piece having the sockets is held in the bench vice and the other laid on it in the exact position. The saw is then placed in each kerf in turn and

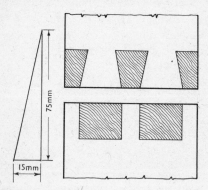

Fig. 2.16 How dovetail slope is set out

Some prefer a slope of 12 mm in 75 mm.

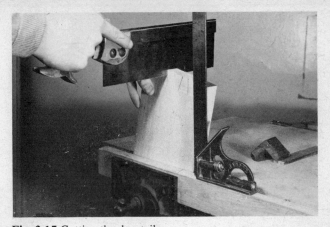

Fig. 2.17 Cutting the dovetails

Take care not to saw past the gauge lines.

Fig. 2.18 Marking out the sockets

The saw is placed in each kerf in turn and is drawn backwards.

is drawn backwards, as shown in Fig. 2.18. The sides of
the sockets are then sawn, the cut being made slightly to
the *waste* side of the marks.

To remove the waste pieces use the coping saw close
up to the gauge line (Fig. 2.19) and finally pare up the
line with the chisel (Fig. 2.20).

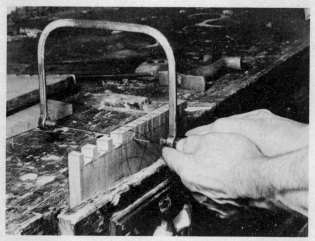

Fig. 2.19 Preliminary removal of waste with coping saw

2.6 Dowelled Joints

Fig. 2.21 shows the dowelled joint in the form in which it
is used to replace the mortise and tenon. Note that a saw-
cut is made along each dowel to allow the surplus glue to
escape when the dowels are knocked in. The holes in both
joining pieces are slightly countersunk, because glue is
awkward to remove cleanly.

B shows the marking out after the wood has been
prepared. The stiles (uprights) and rails (horizontals) are
fixed together temporarily, and the marks are squared

across. In the case of the rails a chisel should be used, and, after separating, they should be squared round on to all four sides. The surplus is then cut off, half from each side. The positions of the dowels are marked as at *C* and

Fig. 2.20 Final removal of waste with chisel

D. When boring, stand at the end of the work so that any tendency for the brace to lean to one side can at once be detected. For 22-mm wood, the usual size of dowel is 9 mm.

Cut up the dowels into suitable lengths and make a saw-cut along each. They can then be glued and stuck

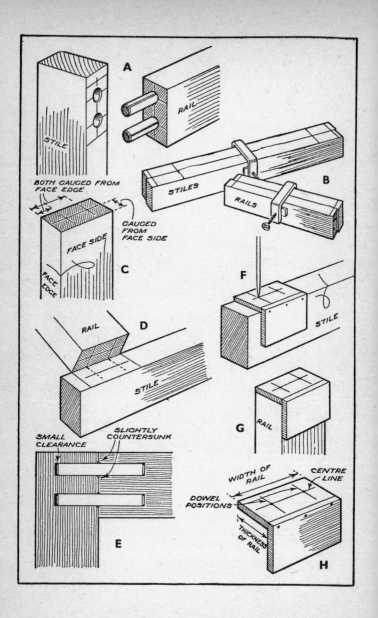

A

STILE

RAIL

BOTH GAUGED FROM FACE EDGE

GAUGED FROM FACE SIDE

STILES

RAILS

B

FACE SIDE

FACE EDGE

C

F

STILE

D

RAIL

STILE

G

RAIL

SMALL CLEARANCE

SLIGHTLY COUNTERSUNK

E

WIDTH OF RAIL

CENTRE LINE

DOWEL POSITIONS

THICKNESS OF RAIL

H

into the ends of the rails and the surplus wiped away. When a fair number of dowelled joints are to be made, it is an economy to make a simple templet, as shown at *H*.

An alternative method is to use a dowelling jig shown in Fig. 2.22. It acts as a bit guide.

Fig. 2.22 The Woden dowelling jig

Another is the Record dowelling jig.

2.7 Mitred Joints

For fitting mouldings together the mitre is essential, but it is also sometimes necessary when jointing up plain wood.

Fig. 2.21 Method of cutting the dowelled joint

    A Completed joint
    B Marking out
    C How ends of rails are gauged
    D Transferring marks to the stiles
    E Section through joint
    F Marking stile with templet
    G Rail being marked with templet
    H Details of templet

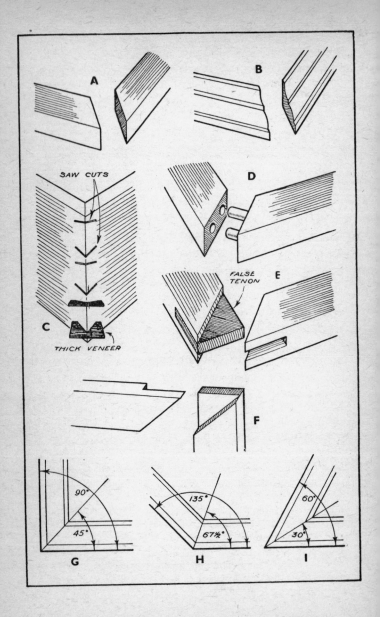

The golden rule to remember is that the line of the mitre always halves the overall angle of the joining pieces. In most cases the last-named are at right angles, and the mitreing angle of 45 degrees is fairly obvious. It is because of this that mitre blocks and similar appliances are made at 45 degrees. When the joining pieces are not at right angles, however, the 45 degrees angle is useless. The idea is shown in Fig. 2.23 at *G*, *H* and *I*.

In its simplest form the surfaces of the mitre are plain, as shown at *A*. It requires merely to be cut with the saw and, if necessary, trimmed on the mitre shooting board. The same joint applied to a moulding is given at *B*. *C* shows a way of strengthening the joint. The joint is cut with plain surfaces (as that illustrated at *A*) and is glued up. When the glue has set, a series of saw-cuts is made dovetail-fashion across the corner and pieces of stout veneer are glued in them. The projecting pieces are levelled down after the glue has set.

At *D* the joint is strengthened with dowels. A somewhat similar but stronger joint is that shown at *E*, in which slots are cut and a loose or false tenon is glued in. If desired, the tenon could be cut in the solid in one of the pieces. When the mitre needs to show at the front only, the halved mitre illustrated at *F* could be cut. The cutting of this is the same as that described for the halved joint.

Fig. 2.23 Types of mitred joints and how angle is found

      A Simple mitre
      B Mitre applied to moulding
      C Strengthening mitre with veneer keys
      D Dowelled mitre
      E Mitre with false tenon
      F Halved mitre
      G, *H*, *I* How mitre line bisects overall angle of joining pieces

2.8 Glue

Resin glue is widely used today. The cold-application urea variety has many advantages, especially on jobs that take a fair time to assemble, there being no risk of chilling. Some glues have a separate water-like hardener, and in this case the glue is applied to one part of the joint and the hardener to the other. Other types have the hardener incorporated in the glue. It is in powder form and requires only to be mixed with water. One advantage is that it is highly water-resistant and is therefore specially suitable for work exposed to damp.

Casein glue is used cold and is more water-resistant than Scotch glue, but it is liable to stain certain hardwoods. As it has no tackiness, it cannot be used for rubbed joints or for the hammer method in veneering.

Polyvinyl acetate glue is used cold and requires no hardener. It can be used for many other substances beside wood—plastics, hardboard, tiles, rubber, etc.

Scotch glue is used to a limited extent and is suitable for any work not liable to become damp. It must be used hot (though it should never be boiled) and calls for care in both its preparation and its use. The cake glue should be broken up into small pieces, steeped in water and left overnight. The next day it is heated in a proper glue kettle (never over a flame) until it is just too hot to be borne on the flesh. Heat the parts being joined so that the glue is not chilled, but take care not to scorch the edges.

3 Workshop Practice

3.1 How to Make a Door

3.1.1 *Flush Doors*

Although the framed-up type of door with separate panel fitting in a groove or rebate is still used to a fair extent, the flush door is becoming increasingly popular.

In its simplest form, the flush door is simply a piece of plywood or laminated board fitted to the cabinet; but this has the disadvantage of showing unsightly layers at the edges, and various means of concealing these have to be adopted. An edging or lipping about 3 mm thick is applied all round, this being planed flush, bevelled or made to project in the form of a bead, as shown in Fig. 3.1(i). One point to note is that plywood is suitable only when the hinges are fixed at the surface. If they are to be at the edge, there are complications, because the screws will not grip well in the layers.

The best form of flush door is that shown in Fig. 3.1(ii), in which the edging is mitred round and both sides are veneered. The veneer thus conceals the edgings. This method is possible only when the door can be veneered *after* the edgings are fixed. If a ready-veneered piece of plywood is used, one of the methods illustrated in (i) must be followed. Note that the grain of the veneer runs at right angles with that of the outer layers of the laminated board.

Both the foregoing methods require the use of stout ply or laminated board, and a useful alternative is to make a thin inner framework and to fix to each side a sheet of 3-mm or 5-mm plywood, as shown in Fig. 3.1(iii). The joints of the framework should preferably be the mortise and tenon, though a halved joint could be used.

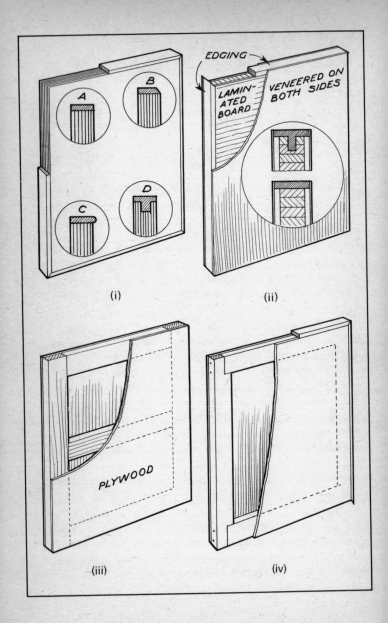

EDGING

A B

LAMIN-
ATED
BOARD

VENEERED ON
BOTH SIDES

C D

(i) (ii)

PLYWOOD

(iii) (iv)

For a very simple door, the construction shown in Fig. 3.1(iv) could be followed. It is somewhat rough and ready but is handy for quick jobs. In all these doors the plywood should be glued to the framework, and if this is properly done no other fixing will be necessary.

3.1.2 *Panelled Doors*

There are many varieties of these, the commonest of which is that with the panel fitting in a rebate, as shown in Fig. 3.2(i). Its advantage is that the rebate is formed by an applied moulding (two types are given), which means that no rebate has to be worked. The simple mortise and tenon or dowelled joint can be used at the corners. The panel is held by a bead at the back. Sometimes it is required to fit the panel in grooves, and this necessitates grooving the rails as in Fig. 3.2(ii).

When it is desired to eliminate joints altogether, the simple method given in Fig. 3.2(iii) can be followed. It does not make a very strong door, but it will do for work not requiring a high standard of finish. A piece of 5-mm plywood is cut to the overall size, and 9-mm or 6-mm strips are glued and nailed around the edges, the joints being merely butted. Note that the front joint is upright and the back one horizontal. Another variation of the same thing is that shown in Fig. 3.2(iv), in which strips of 12-mm stuff are glued together. Those at the back are 6 mm narrower than those at the front, so that a rebate is formed in which the panel can fit.

Fig. 3.1 Various types of flush doors

    (i) Door of thick plywood with lipping
    (ii) Edged and veneered laminated board
    (iii) Framework with glued-on ply panels
    (iv) Simple notched framework with ply panels

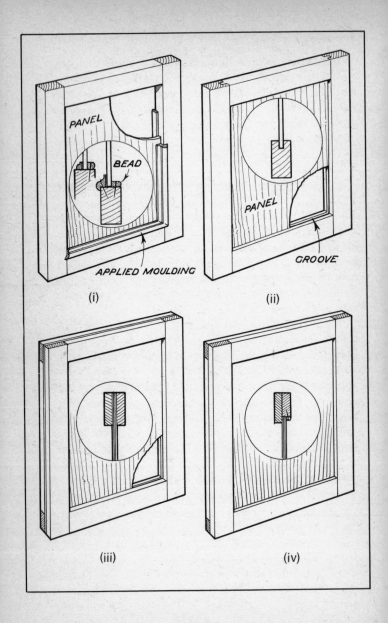

PANEL

BEAD

APPLIED MOULDING

(i)

PANEL

GROOVE

(ii)

(iii)

(iv)

3.1.3 *Making the Door*

As an example of the procedure, let us suppose that a door has to be made to fit a cupboard, the inside size of which is 46 cm by 30 cm as shown in Fig. 3.3(i). To allow for trimming the door should be about 1·5 mm full in length and width, which means that the stiles will be marked to 46·15 cm. The way in which the parts are fixed together whilst marking out has already been dealt with in Fig. 2.13, page 65.

The joints having been cut, each should be fitted individually and marked so that it can be replaced in the same position. The whole thing is then tried together to see that it is free from winding. This is done by holding the framework in line with the eye, when the near and far rails should appear parallel. Fig. 3.3(ii) shows a door in winding. The trouble is due to faults in the joints, and may be caused by either the mortise or tenon being cut at an angle (*A*), or by one or the other not being parallel with the side (*B*). The remedy is obvious.

It can now be glued up. Both mortise and tenon are glued, and the whole is cramped together. A small door such as that we are dealing with can be tested for squareness with an ordinary try-square (Fig. 3.3(iii)). In a larger one it is better to use the diagonal strip method, in which a lath of wood is pointed at one end and placed diagonally across the door and the length marked. When reversed into the opposite corners, it should show the same length (Fig. 3.3(v)).

When the glue has set, the projecting ends of the stiles

Fig. 3.2 Framed-up doors in various forms

    (i) Door with applied moulding and bead
  (ii) Panel grooved in
 (iii) Simple door with 'framework' glued on
 (iv) Simple way of making door with rebate

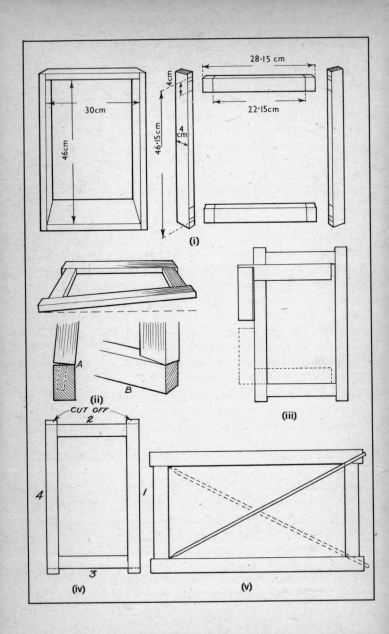

30cm

46cm

46·15cm

4cm

4cm

28·15 cm

22·15cm

(i)

A

B

(ii)

(iii)

CUT OFF

2

4

1

3

(iv)

(v)

are sawn off (Fig. 3.3(iv)). The hingeing edge (right hand) is planed true and the top edge trimmed so that it fits accurately against the cupboard. The bottom edge follows, and finally the opening edge (left hand) is fitted. The notes on hingeing given in §3.4 should be read, because it will be seen that this opening edge has to be planed at a slight angle. There should not be any gaps around any of the edges, but the door must not bind anywhere. Remember that, if the job is to be polished later, the polish will build up a certain thickness.

The panel should never be glued in, as this may cause splitting if in solid wood. Incidentally, it is always better to leave fixing until after polishing, because it is awkward to work the rubber into the corners. In the case of a grooved-in panel, it is advisable if possible to stain and polish before assembling, so that in the event of shrinkage there will not be any edges of white, unstained wood showing.

3.2 Making a Drawer

3.2.1 *A Dovetailed Drawer*

The best way of making a drawer is to dovetail it. For the usual run of drawers, a thickness of 22 mm or 19 mm is suitable for the front. The sides and back can be 9 mm, and the bottom 5 mm. The latter is nowadays usually of plywood and is held by a grooved moulding made specially for the purpose.

Plane the lower edge of the front true and trim one end

Fig. 3.3 Stages in making a framed-up door

    (i) How sizes are calculated
   (ii) Door in winding with (*A* and *B*) likely causes
  (iii) Testing door with square
  (iv) Order in which edges are planed
   (v) Testing door with diagonal strip

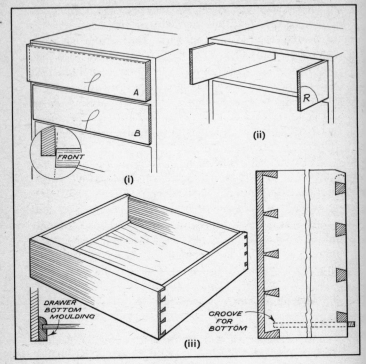

Fig. 3.4 How dovetailed drawer is made

    (i) Fitting the front
    (ii) Sides being fitted
    (iii) Completed drawer and setting out of dovetails

so that it makes a perfect fit with the side of the cabinet. If
it is placed in position, as at *A*, Fig. 3.4(i), it is easy to
test. Mark the exact length and width, and trim first the
end and then the top until it makes a close fit. It is a good
plan to make a *slightly* tapering fit, so that the inner face
can just be entered into the opening. The taper must,
however, be very small—not more than the thickness of a

shaving. *B*, Fig. 3.4(i), shows the front at this stage. The inset shows in exaggeration the taper.

The sides follow and, the bottom edges being planed straight, the ends are made square, both of exactly the same length. A gauge is set to slightly more than the width and the top edges are planed until each side makes a hand-tight fit, as shown in Fig. 3.4(ii). The front edges should be marked *R* and *L* so that there is no confusion when assembling. The back is treated similarly to the front, except that the edges are square and it is narrower than the front. The reason for this can be seen in Fig. 3.4(iii), which shows how the back stands *above* the bottom and is set down slightly at the top.

It is usual for the bottom to rest in a groove in the drawer front, and it is necessary, therefore, for the bottom dovetail at the front to be low so that the groove occurs *within* the dovetail; otherwise, a gap will show at the ends. When glueing up, place a piece of wood over the joints and strike this so that the wood is not bruised, and to avoid splitting the corners. Test for squareness with the try-square and put aside.

When the glue has set, clean up the joints and fit the drawer. Make sure where the drawer sticks before taking off any shavings. The moulding is now glued in, and finally the bottom is passed in from the back and screwed to the back. If solid wood is used, the bottom should be allowed to project about 6 mm at the back, so that in the event of shrinkage it can later be pushed forward. This is unnecessary in the case of plywood. A good lubricant for drawers is candle grease, but this should not be applied until after the work has been polished.

3.2.2 *A Simple Method*
In place of dovetails, a simple lapped joint can be used at the front, as shown in Fig. 3.5. It is not so strong as a

dovetailed drawer, but it serves its purpose for a cheap
job. The back fits in grooves. The preliminary fitting is
the same as that already described, except that the back is
cut short by an amount equal to the thickness of wood
left at the bottom of the two grooves. Fig. 3.6 shows how
the wood is marked out with the gauge. To avoid grooving the front the drawer bottom moulding can be fixed

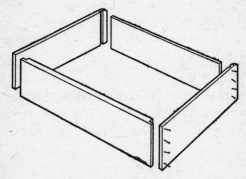

Fig. 3.5 Simple drawer construction

> The front corners are lapped and the back ones
> grooved.

here as well as at the sides. The whole thing is put
together with glue and nails, the last-named being driven
in dovetail-fashion and punched in.

3.3 How to Fit a Lock

There are two kinds of locks used in furniture: those
requiring merely to be screwed on and those which have
to be let in. The latter kind are by far the better because
they are much neater and they take up no space in the
drawer, or whatever it may be. Some locks are made so
that they can be used on either a drawer or a door, the

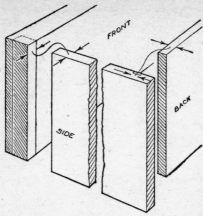

Fig. 3.6 Drawer construction

How parts are gauged when making a simple drawer.

hole for the key being cut in duplicate. Others are made specifically for the one or the other and must be ordered accordingly. One other point is that a door may close on either right or left hand, and care must be taken to select the correct one. An example of a 'left-hand' lock is given at *A*, Fig. 3.7. This could also be used for a drawer.

3.3.1 *A Drawer Lock*

First square down a line in the centre of the front from the top edge and set a gauge to the centre of the pin of the lock from its top edge as at *B*, Fig. 3.7. With it mark the front at the line. This gives the position of the pin. Select a bit that will make a hole slightly less in diameter than the top rounded part of the escutcheon and bore right through the front as at *C*. Place the escutcheon in position and tap it lightly with the hammer so that it makes an indentation (*D*). Then, fixing the drawer on the bench, cut down the sides with keyhole saw (*E*) and chisel away the waste. The escutcheon can be tapped in flush.

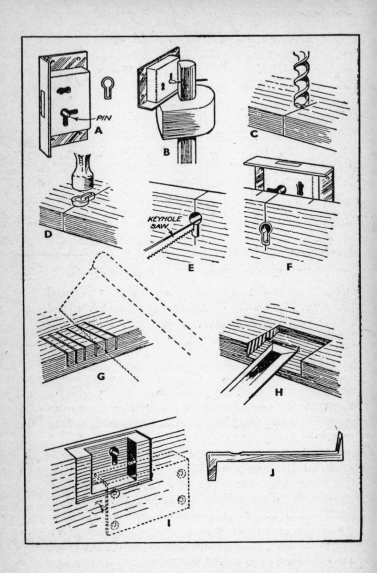

The next step is to mark where the wood has to be cut away to enable the body of the lock to be let in. This is done by holding the lock with the pin opposite the centre line (this is squared across the top edge) and marking the sides as at *F*. These lines are squared down inside, and a gauge is used to mark both the thickness and the depth.

When cutting away the waste, make a saw-cut at each line, as at *G*, and a series of cuts between to cut up the grain. Cut down the sides with the chisel and pare away the waste as at *H*. This will enable the lock to be placed in position so that the outer plate can be marked round. Sometimes only the top part of the plate is let in flush, and this certainly saves time, though a much neater job results when the back is also let in. The sides are cut round with the chisel and the waste is carefully pared away.

When the screws have been driven in, the position of the mortise to allow the bolt to be shot home can be marked. This is done by smearing a little dark paste (such as the dirty oil from an oilstone) on the top of the bolt. The key is then turned and the drawer pushed right home. If the key is turned, the bolt will leave an impression on the upper rail of the chest. A drawer lock chisel is handy

---

Fig. 3.7 Stages in fitting a lock

    A Lock suitable for door or drawer. Note also escutcheon
    B Setting gauge to pin
    C Boring for escutcheon
    D Tapping escutcheon to make indentation
    E Sawing sides of keyhole
    F Marking position of body of lock
    G Preliminary sawing out
    H Paring away waste
    I Notch for lock completed
    J Drawer lock chisel

to cut the mortise with; it is shown at *J*. Otherwise, a short chisel or even a bradawl can be used.

When a box lock is fitted, the general procedure for fixing the lock is similar. To enable the link-plate to be fixed it is placed in position on the lock. It will be found to have a couple of spikes at the top side, and by closing the lid and thumping it the spikes will enter the lid and will rise with it when the latter is opened.

3.4 How to Fit Hinges

There are a great many varieties of hinges, each designed for a special purpose. The simplest kind is that intended to be screwed straight on to the door without being recessed, and this usually has a decorative shape to take off its crudeness. It is not, however, specially strong, because the whole weight of the door falls on the screws, and a much neater type is the butt hinge. This is intended to be recessed into the wood, so that the hinge, in resting in its recess, is supported to a large extent quite apart from the screws. These can be obtained in a wide range of sizes, and in both brass and iron.

Similar in type is the back flap. The leaves are, however, much wider, being practically square, and they are used for such jobs as bureau falls. Another type, known as the T hinge, is used for outdoor work for hanging large doors. It does not require to be let in.

3.4.1 *The Butt Hinge*
The position in which a hinge is fixed depends on the way the door is to be hung. For instance, at *A*, Fig. 3.8, the door closes *over* the sides of the cupboard, and in this case the hinge is recessed into the back of the door and the front edge of the side. At *B* the door is contained *between* the sides, and the hinges are let into the edge of

the door and the inner side of the cupboard. One point to note here is that the outer or closing edge of the door must be taken off at a slight angle, as shown, because otherwise it will bind when opened. Whenever a single door is hinged, the hinges are fixed at the right-hand side, unless there is some special reason to the contrary. The usual way of hingeing a box is given at *C*, the hinges being let into the edges of both lid and box.

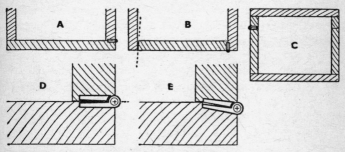

Fig. 3.8 Sections through hinged joints

    A Door closes over cupboard sides
    B Door contained between sides
    C Box hinge
    D Hinge let equally into door and cupboard
    E Hinge let wholly into door

As a rule, both leaves of the hinge are let in equally as at *D*, and, since most hinges when closed are thicker at the knuckle than at the outer edges, the extent to which they are let in is measured from the knuckle, because it is here that the whole pivoting takes place. In every case, then, the centre of the knuckle is worked to, both in the depth and in the distance in from the edge. *D* shows how this centre lines up with both the outer faces, and with the crack between the door and the cupboard.

In some cases it is an advantage to let the hinge wholly

into the door as at *E*. Even in this, however, a sloping recess is cut in the cupboard, so that the edge of the leaf is let in. This not only makes a neater finish but also strengthens it. Note that only the edge is let in (*E*): the knuckle simply rests on the surface.

3.4.2 *Fitting the Hinge*
Assuming that the hinges of a door are to be let in equally in both leaves, the first step is to mark the positions in which they are to be fitted. As a general guide, they can be fixed their own length from the end of the door, though this may have to be varied in special circumstances. Place the hinge in position, mark both ends with a pricker or sharp pencil and square the lines across, as at *C*, Fig. 3.9.

The depth and distance in from the edge are now gauged. If two gauges are available, it is an advantage, so that they can remain set for marking the cupboard; otherwise, resetting will be necessary. *A* and *B*, Fig. 3.9, show how the marker points to the centre of the pin in both cases. Mark both the edge and the face of the door, taking care not to overrun the marks.

With a fine saw, cut each line and make a series of cuts between, as at *D*, so that the grain is cut up short. Now tap the chisel downwards at each end (see dotted lines at *E* and also at the back, placing the chisel just inside the gauge line. The waste is pared away and a final cut made right on the gauge line. When the bottom is quite smooth, fix the hinge with a couple of screws only.

Fig. 3.9 Stages in fitting butt hinges

      A Gauge set to depth
      B Setting gauge to thickness
      C Squaring in position of hinges
      D Preliminary sawing
      E Chiselling recess
      F Transferring marks to cupboard

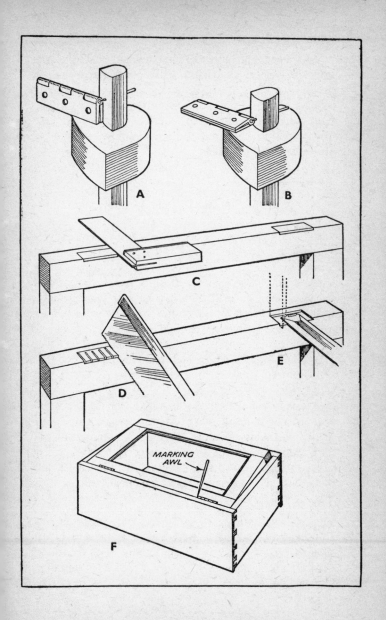

A

B

C

D

E

MARKING
AWL

F

To transfer the marks to the cupboard place the door in position as at *F*, and mark with a marking awl or sharp pencil. The recesses are cut and a single screw is driven into each hinge. If any adjustment is needed when the door is closed, a screw can be driven into another hole. The general rule is to put in all remaining screws after the whole has been polished.

3.5 Veneering

Veneering is not difficult to do and does not call for much in the way of special appliances, but it is essential that the work is done properly if the result is to be a success. The groundwork must be sound and be properly prepared. Solid, straight-grained mahogany or American white-wood is the best ground. Deal is not recommended, because the resin in it prevents the glue from gripping well and it is liable to soak up too much of the glue. If it is used, a best-quality grade free from knots should be selected, and, to seal the grain, it should be sized with glue thinned down with water. Size should also be used when end grain is veneered, though this is never a very satisfactory thing to do.

An excellent material is laminated board. Plywood, too, gives good results if a good grade is selected. A poor quality is useless, because there are invariably internal faults which eventually show through to the surface. The veneer should be laid with its grain at right angles with that of the ply, otherwise cracks may develop.

3.5.1 *The Pull of Veneer*
Veneer always tends to pull the groundwork hollow. Consequently, the ideal arrangement is to veneer both sides so that the pull is equalised. For such a piece of work as a flush door, this is really essential because there is no supporting framework.

When the veneer is to be laid on one side only, it should be put on the heart side of the groundwork. Fig. 3.10 explains this. A board, if it is going to twist at all, tends to pull so that the ends turn away from the centre of the log, this being due to the main shrinkage taking place around the annual rings. If, therefore, the veneer is laid on the heart side, the forces are opposed as shown. Another precaution is to damp the groundwork on the underside when veneering.

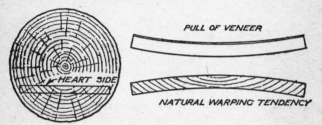

PULL OF VENEER

HEART SIDE

NATURAL WARPING TENDENCY

Fig. 3.10 How pulling tendency is minimised

The warping tendency is opposed to the pull of the veneer, the latter being laid on the heart side.

Various glues can be used, but the initial preparation of the groundwork is the same in all cases.

The groundwork is first prepared by planing it dead true. To remove the plane-marks, and to roughen the surface to form a key for the glue, a toothing plane is then worked over the entire surface diagonally, first in one direction and then in the other, as shown in Fig. 3.11. The cutter of this toothing plane is practically upright and is scored so that the 'edge' presents a series of sharp points. If a plane is not available, a piece of the coarsest glasspaper can be wrapped round a flat block of wood, care being taken not to dub over the edges. If the groundwork is of softwood, it is then sized and set aside to dry. All dust must be carefully brushed away.

The veneer is next cut to size, and, assuming that it has to cover the entire groundwork, it is cut about 12 mm full all round. A chisel can be used for cutting, the veneer being pressed down on to a flat board with a straight-edge, as shown in Fig. 3.12.

Fig. 3.11 Use of the toothing plane

It is worked diagonally, first in one direction and then in the other.

Today veneer is generally laid by means of a press, if available. The groundwork is given an even coat of adhesive, the veneer placed in position and a sheet of newspaper put on top to prevent any squeezed-out glue from sticking to the press. Pressure is then applied and the work left until the adhesive has hardened. Few home workshops have a press, however, and the alternative of a caul is used. This is a flat panel of wood slightly larger than the work, its purpose being to force the veneer into close contact with the groundwork, and necessitates the use of several cramps. When the work is quite small the cramps can be tightened directly over the caul, but for work of any size it is necessary to use two or more pairs of cross-bearers, as shown in Fig. 3.13. These bearers are

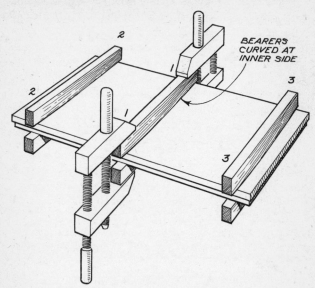

Fig. 3.12 How caul is clamped down in caul veneering

Fig. 3.13 Cutting veneer with chisel

slightly curved at their inner edges, so that when the cramps are applied at the ends the pressure is felt at the centre first, thus forcing surplus glue outwards. Unless this is done, glue may be trapped in the middle, making it impossible for the veneer to be in close contact with the groundwork. For the same reason, the centre cross-bearers are put on first, as shown by the numbers. Note that when both sides of the groundwork are to be veneered the two veneers are laid simultaneously.

At this stage we have to consider the adhesive to be used. Resin glue, P.V.A., casein and Scotch glue can all be used with the caul or press methods, but in the case of Scotch glue the caul has to be heated thoroughly before-hand. The heat liquefies the glue and enables it to be pressed out.

There is another way of veneering still used occasion-ally, the hammer method, but this can be used only when Scotch glue is the adhesive, the reason being that this has a natural tackiness which holds the veneers in its early stage of setting. This tackiness is largely absent in other adhesives. Hammer veneering does not carry any special advantages, except that it does not need a large number of cramps. The veneering hammer is shown in Fig. 3.14, and its purpose is to force out surplus glue at the edges and to bring the veneer into close contact with the groundwork.

The glue must not be too thick. When thoroughly warm, it should run down freely without breaking into drops from the brush when the latter is held a few inches from the pot. Apply the glue to both the veneer and the groundwork, and place the former in position, smoothing it out with the hands. It does not matter if the glue chills during the operation.

To heat the glue an ordinary domestic flat-iron is used. Do not make it too hot. It should give just a comfortable warmth when held a few inches from the cheek. With a swab damp about one-half of the veneer. This is to prevent the veneer and glue from being scorched; but avoid a surplus of water. Pass the iron over the surface, and then proceed to press out the glue with the veneering hammer (see Fig. 3.14), working the latter with a zig-zag movement from the centre outwards. The hammer is shown in use in Fig. 3.15.

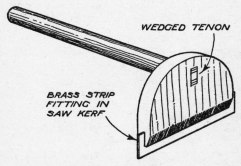

WEDGED TENON

BRASS STRIP FITTING IN SAW KERF

Fig. 3.14 Details of veneering hammer

The brass strip can be from 130 mm–150 mm long and about 1·5 mm thick. The handle is about 230 mm long.

When the one half has been completed, the other can be dealt with similarly. To test whether the veneer is properly down tap the surface with the fingernails. It should give a solid feeling. Wipe off any surplus glue with the swab, and cut off the overhang by turning the whole thing upside down on a flat board and cutting round with a chisel. The groundwork must be pressed tightly down.

Allow plenty of time for the glue to set—at least twenty-four hours. A scraper is used for cleaning up, after which glasspaper is used, first Fine 2 and then No. 1½.

Sometimes in a wide piece, or when two pieces are being matched, a joint has to be made. First lay the one piece and then the other so that it overlaps the first by about 10 mm. Place a straight-edge along the overlap, fix

Fig. 3.15 Pressing down with veneering hammer

It is worked from the centre outwards so that the glue is squeezed out at the edges.

it with a couple of thumbscrews and make a single cut right the way along, as shown in Fig. 3.16, so that both thicknesses are cut through. Remove the straight-edge and peel away the one piece of waste. To get at the other the veneer must be raised, as shown in Fig. 3.17. It is then heated and rubbed down finally, a piece of gummed

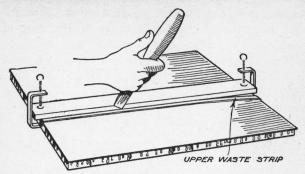

Fig. 3.16 Making a joint in veneer

The chisel cuts through both thicknesses.

tape being stuck over the joint to prevent it from opening as the glue dries out.

When joints are needed in veneer to be laid with the caul or press, the edges of the veneer are trimmed to a clean joint on the shooting board. The veneer should overhang the upper part of the board no more than 2 mm–3 mm, and a batten is placed on top of the veneer to prevent it from buckling and to hold it down. A piece of

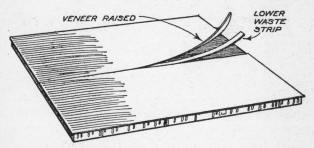

Fig. 3.17 Jointing in veneer

The veneer is raised to allow the lower waste strip to be peeled away.

gummed tape is stuck over the joint to hold it together, after which the whole is regarded as a single sheet of veneer and laid in the way already described.

When a panel is to be cross-banded around the sides, the main part of the veneer is cut a trifle small, and, after laying, a cutting gauge is set to the width of the banding and is worked all round. The waste is then peeled away, as shown in Fig. 3.18. The veneer for the banding can

Fig. 3.18 Laying cross-banding

Gauging around edges and removing waste.

also be cut with the cutting gauge set a trifle full. The edge is first planed on the shooting board, as shown in Fig. 3.19, a straight-edge being pressed down on top to prevent buckling. The gauge can be used first from one side and then from the other.

When laying the cross-banding, any jointing, such as the corner mitres and butt joints in the length, is done as the work proceeds. The pane of an ordinary hammer can be used for rubbing down. Gummed tape is stuck over all joints. When cleaning up a cross-banded panel, the scraper should be held at an angle so that there is less tendency for the grain to tear out.

3.6 Wood Finishing

A finish of some sort is desirable on any piece of wood-work, partly because bare wood rapidly becomes soiled

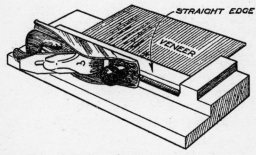

Fig. 3.19 Trimming edges of veneer

The straight-edge or batten prevents the veneer from buckling.

with use and partly because a polish serves to seal the grain.

Sometimes the polish is applied directly to the wood but occasionally it is first stained. There is a tendency nowadays to eliminate the staining and, if the same kind of wood is used throughout, the result is quite successful. Sometimes it happens that different kinds of, say, oak have been used, and the tone therefore varies. In this case a stain is desirable so that the whole tones down to a common shade.

One form of finish generally known as a varnish stain has the effect of colouring and giving a shine in one operation, but it is not recommended for good work because the colouring matter is contained in the varnish and has the effect of hiding the grain.

3.6.1 *Stains*

There are many excellent proprietary stains on the market and the reader cannot do better than use these. Instructions on their use are supplied with the stains, and these should be followed implicitly. Also, the following finish should be taken into account, as some stains are incompatible with the finish. Here again, the instructions given with the finish should be followed, otherwise there may be trouble owing to the polish not drying or to oil soaking through and causing it to become dull.

Stains can also be made up by the reader himself. Aniline dyes give good results, and various shades can be mixed together to produce any special colour. They are in powder form and can be obtained soluble in methylated spirit, turps or water. A thorough mixing is essential, and they should be allowed to stand for several hours before use. A little French polish can be added to the spirit stain to act as a binder. The spirit stain is not so liable to raise the grain as the water variety.

A cheap stain can be made from Vandyke crystals. These are dissolved in warm water, the amount depending on the shade required. A little glue size is added while it is still warm to bind it. It gives a medium brown shade. Another good stain is made from asphaltum. This is dissolved in turpentine and, after straining, a little gold size is added. It gives a brown shade, which is useful for imitating oak or walnut and is of value chiefly for deal.

Oak can be darkened by fuming, and, since no liquid is applied, the grain is not raised. The work is placed in a cupboard with a close-fitting door, and the ammonia (known as 'point eight eighty') is poured into a saucer. The time it remains in the cupboard depends on the shade required and the size of the cupboard. It may vary from fifteen minutes up to several hours. Great care must be taken not to bend over the ammonia because the fumes are very strong. The work is best done out in the open. Since some varieties of oak are more susceptible to the fumes than others (American oak is scarcely affected), it is important that the same kind of oak be used throughout.

Alternatively, any of the proprietary stains can be used, or those made up with aniline dyes. Permanganate of potash is sometimes used, but it is not permanent, the colour gradually changing in the course of time.

An excellent plan for mahogany is to use bichromate of potash, which darkens the wood by chemical action rather than by staining. This is in crystal form, and the crystals are placed in water, which will gradually turn a reddish-orange shade. It is applied to the wood by daylight and allowed to dry out. The wood will turn a brown shade free from the objectionable reddish shade often seen in mahogany furniture. A yellowish dust is left on the surface, and this is wiped off before polishing. Aniline dyes or proprietary stains can also be used. Walnut is usually best left without staining, though any of the marketed stains or aniline dyes can be used.

It is inevitable that water and spirit stains will raise the grain to a certain extent, and to minimise this the work should first be damped with water and allowed to dry. The surface can then be glasspapered smooth. When the stain is applied, the grain will rise to a small extent only.

Brushes are needed for staining, also a rag. The stain is applied *with* the grain, and the edges should be kept alive so that patches are avoided. To get rid of brush-marks the rag is soaked in the stain, wrung out and wiped over the surface in long, even strokes. When staining a piece of panelling such as a door, the panels should be stained first. Start at one side, not the middle, so that there is only one edge to keep alive. Now stain the framing, carrying the stain cleanly up to the joints of the horizontal rails and finishing off at the uprights, as shown in Fig. 3.20.

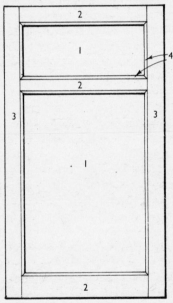

Fig. 3.20 Staining a door

Figures show order in which parts should be stained.

The mouldings are picked in lastly with a small brush. Generally it is better to give two weak coats of stain rather than one strong one. The first must dry out thoroughly and be lightly glasspapered smooth before the second is applied.

One point to note (and this applies equally to polishing) is that, when possible, the parts should be separated. For instance, panels are more easily dealt with before being fixed in the framework. If this is not possible, the edges should be stained before fixing, so that in the event of shrinkage there will not be any white gaps as the panel draws out of the grooves.

If for any reason a part of the work is of too dark a shade, it can be bleached with oxalic acid. This is a powder, and it is dissolved in warm water, about 1 oz (28 g) of acid to $\frac{1}{2}$ pt (284 ml) of water. It is applied to the work, several times if necessary. Sometimes a swab soaked in the acid can be left on the work if the dark patch is local. Afterwards, it should be well washed with water to get rid of the acid, as the latter may have a bad effect upon any polish to be applied later. Since the acid is a poison, care should be taken to wash the fingers afterwards.

Some proprietary stains have preservative qualities that make them specially useful for outdoor woodwork, and these should certainly be used for jobs liable to be exposed to the weather. For floorboards, the Vandyke crystals already mentioned are suitable and have the advantage of cheapness. If the floor is not new, it should be washed thoroughly first with warm water, in which a few lumps of soda have been dissolved, to get rid of any grease.

3.6.2 *Wax Polish*
A polish that dates back for centuries and has recently become popular is wax polish. It gives a somewhat dull, eggshell finish, which looks especially well on oak and walnut. It has two great advantages: it is inexpensive and is easy to apply.

Two kinds of wax are available, yellow and white, and

the reader can decide which is the more suitable for his purpose. For a light wood that is to be kept as light as possible, the white is the better. It should be shredded into a tin, just covered with turpentine and allowed to dissolve. The process can be quickened by standing the tin in hot water. Never place it over a flame; it will inevitably flare up. When ready, it should be in the form of a paste of thin consistency, and it is applied either with a brush or a rag. Many excellent proprietary polishes are also available.

The wood must be quite dry, and, in the event of its having been stained with an oil stain, the latter should be fixed with two coats of French polish. It is a good plan to rub over the surface with a rag to remove any traces of oil. At least twenty-four hours should be allowed for the turpentine to evaporate, after which the whole can be polished with a rubber free from fluff. Probably the first application will not produce much of a shine, but it helps to body up the work with French polish before applying wax.

3.6.3 *Various Polishes*

There are several proprietary polishes that give excellent results, ranging from a brilliant gloss to an eggshell effect. These are mostly brush-applied and dry with an extremely hard surface, which can be burnished with a superfine polishing compound. Many of them have the advantage of being damp-, spirit- and heat-resistant, a special advantage for such items as table-tops. The instructions supplied need to be carefully followed because, although simple to apply, there may be complications in accordance with any stain or filler previously given.

One of these finishes is polyurethane lacquer, which has good wear-resistant qualities. It may be a two-can type, the base and the hardener, which dries only after the two have been mixed; or the one-can type used straight as it is from the container. There are varieties for brushing, spraying or fadding, and it is essential that only recommended stains and fillers are used.

Another finish is plastic lacquer based on synthetic resin. It consists of the lacquer proper, a hardener and thinners. Generally the best effect is obtained by diluting the lacquer with the thinners (in addition to using the hardener) and applying two or more coats rather than one full-strength coat. When thoroughly hard, the surface is lightly rubbed down with superfine glasspaper and finally burnished with the compound supplied. A brilliant gloss can be built up, but if preferred it can be dulled down with the finest grade steel wool lubricated with wax polish.

Cellulose lacquer can also be used. According to type, it may be brush-, spray- or rubber-applied. Here again, the instructions supplied with it should be followed.

A finish that has become popular is teak oil, and this has the advantage of easy application. It can be renewed at any time, and an attractive dull gloss can be built up. If used over a surface previously in use, it is advisable to rub down with turps substitute before application. Teak oil can be used on almost any wood.

3.6.4 *French Polish*

This is a job calling for considerable experience, and the reader is advised not to make a good piece of work his first effort.

The first steps after the wood has been stained is to give two coats of French polish as a sealer, then fill in the grain. Proprietary fillers can be obtained, and they give excellent results. The instructions given on the container should be followed. Special care must be taken to clean

out corners, mouldings and so on, and a little piece of
stick is handy for this. The work is set aside to harden. In
all stages of French polishing, allow plenty of time between each process.

A piece of flour-grade glasspaper is next rubbed over
the surface to remove any filler and to smooth it. The
necessity of wiping off the surplus in the preliminary
filling is appreciated at this stage. The French polish can
be obtained ready-made.

The rubber is made up of a little wad of cotton wool
with the skin removed. It is charged with polish and
moulded into a pear shape. A piece of fine muslin is used
to cover it, and it should be so wrapped round it that the
sole is free from all creases. Every time the rubber needs
recharging the cover should be taken off, the cotton wool
placed over the top of the bottle and the latter inverted.
The rubber should exude a *little* polish when pressed, but
on no account should it be too fully charged.

In the opening stages, the polish can be applied a little
more generously because it is bound to soak into the
grain. Work the rubber with a circular motion, taking
special care at the corners. Polishers have a saying that
if the corners are attended to the middle will take care
of itself. Work out the rubber until it is dry and then
go over another part of the job. It is always an
advantage to polish several articles at the same time,
because some can be hardening whilst others are being
dealt with.

After a couple of hours or so, the surface is rubbed
lightly down with the finest worn glasspaper. Now give a
second coat of polish, continuing the circular motion (as
shown in Fig. 3.21, and work the rubber until it is
practically dry. If it begins to drag, a single spot of
linseed oil can be applied to the sole with the finger.
Avoid too much oil, however, because it prevents a high

gloss and it has all to be worked out later. Once again, set the work aside and proceed with another part of the job. The time allowed between the successive rubbings is most important.

Proceeding in this way a good body will gradually be built up. When a fair shine has been attained, the circular movement is changed for long, even strokes *with* the grain. Before the application of each coat, rub the surface down with the worn glasspaper.

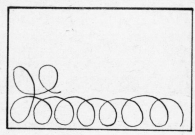

Fig. 3.21 French polishing

The circular path of the rubber when bodying up.

The final stage is known as spiriting off, and it is one that requires the utmost care. Make a fresh rubber and sprinkle on the cotton wool a couple of drops of methylated spirit—no more. Work this well into the cotton wool so that it is evenly distributed and, wrapping round the cover, work it along the surface in long, even strokes. The object of this is to remove all traces of oil and to burnish the surface. After a few rubs the sole of the rubber will be greasy with oil, and the cover should be moved so that a fresh, clean part covers the sole. Work the rubber until it is quite dry, and if the process has been done properly a brilliant shine will be the result. When the polish has hardened, the process can be repeated. Note that only the slightest trace of spirit should be used.

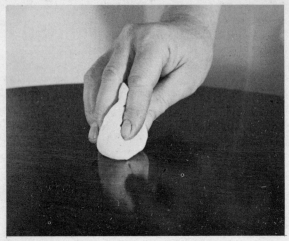

Fig. 3.22 How French-polishing rubber is held

It should be moulded to a pear shape.

If the rubber is really damp, it will drag off the polish and ruin the work.

Fig. 3.22 shows how the rubber is held. A pear shape allows a pointed corner at the front which will work into the corners. When finished with for the night, rubbers should be kept in an air-tight tin.

4 Outdoor Woodwork, etc.

4.1 Work Bench

An essential feature of a bench is that it is rigid and able
to stand up to the racking strains it is necessarily sub-
jected to. The top, too, must be firm and thick enough to
resist bending, and solid so that it can stand up to heavy
chopping work, such as mortising. The height may have
to be adapted to suit the stature of the individual user; 89

Fig. 4.1 Useful bench with well top and drawer and shelf
accommodation

cm is about right for the average man. Length may be a
matter of the space available, but it should be as long as is
practicable. Depth is also a matter of convenience. Again,
make it as large as space will allow.

The well-type top is recommended because it enables
the many small tools in constant use to be left in the well,
where they are handy. A metal vice is fitted, and an
adjustable stop is incorporated at the head, this being
held by a wing nut tightened over a washer. The wide
front rail (generally called the apron piece) has two

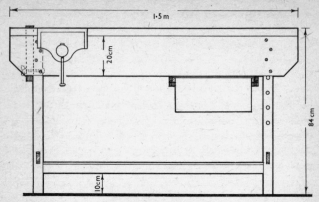

Fig. 4.2 Front elevation

advantages. Being grooved to fit over the legs, it effectually prevents side racking and enables a thinner top to be used, as it resists bending strain. Big tools and appliances can be kept on the large shelf and small ones in the drawer. The latter should not be fitted with a stop to

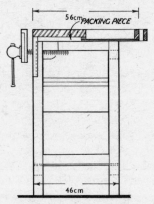

Fig. 4.3 Side elevation

prevent its being pulled right out, because for some jobs it is desirable to remove it.

Figs. 4.2 and 4.3 give the main sizes, and Fig. 4.4 the method of making the main framework. The two end frames are put together with through mortise and tenon joints, these being wedged from outside. Top back and both bottom rails have stub tenons to fit into the legs, and long bolts are passed right through to engage with nuts let into the rails, as shown in Figs. 4.4 and 4.5, so that the whole is held tightly together. It also enables the whole

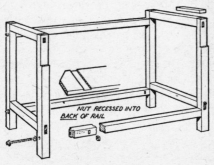

Fig. 4.4 Details of construction

thing to be taken down and stacked if it is necessary to store the bench at any time.

Begin by making the two end frames. Use a hardwood if possible, such as beech or oak. Squares of 5-cm section can be obtained and require only to be planed true. To make sure that all are marked alike they should be fixed together side by side temporarily and the mortise positions squared across all. Those for the top side rails are at the extreme tops of the legs, and the lower ones stand up 15·6 cm from the floor. As the tenons pass right through, the marks must be squared round to the opposite faces. Additional marks are squared across at the

Fig. 4.5 How bolts hold front and back legs to rails

outside about 5 mm outside the other lines. The mortises
are sloped back to these outer lines so that, when driven
in, the wedges cause the tenons to have a dovetail grip.

Note that the blind mortises for front and back rails
are below those for the sides, a gap of 6 mm being left
between the two so that the shelf of 6-mm ply can fit
beneath the side rails but *above* those at front and back.
Mortises for top back rail are immediately below those
for the top side rails.

Glue up the end frames independently, cramping them
and driving wedges into saw-cuts made in the tenons (Fig.
4.6). Level the joints when the glue has set and cut back

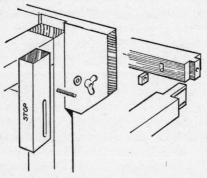

Fig. 4.6 Method of fitting stop

the front legs at the top (Fig. 4.4). The mortises for front and back rails are about 19 mm deep only. The length of the tenons is slightly less than this. The fit should be hand-tight, and the parts should be held together temporarily with a cramp and a hole bored through from outside right into the tenon and about 76 mm into the rails. Use a 9·5-mm bit for 9·5-mm bolts. At the back of the rail a recess is cut to take a nut. This recess must obviously be in line with the bored hole, and in size it should allow the nut to go in freely without being able to turn round. Obviously the bored hole must extend well beyond the notch so that the bolt, having engaged the nut, can pass beyond.

Having fitted the rails into the legs, the apron rail is fitted, this being grooved at the back as in Fig. 4.4 to fit over the cut-back part at the top of the legs. Fix with four stout screws at each leg. Note, however, that it stands up beyond the top of the legs by the thickness of the packing piece (see Figs. 4.3 and 4.6). This latter is decided by the depth of the well at the back of the bench in relation to the thickness of the top.

The whole thing having been put together, the shelf can be fitted, the corners being cut to fit around the legs. The parts can then be separated and the shelf slipped in. The main top should preferably be 38 mm thick and in hardwood, but thinner stuff can be used if necessary. To form the well a piece of 6-mm ply is screwed beneath the main top with a strip sandwiched between, as shown in Fig. 4.3. A 22-mm backing is screwed up from beneath, and a tool rack is screwed on at the back, this consisting of a 12-mm strip with distance pieces between. The ends are filled in with sloping, wedge-shaped pieces, these having the advantage of enabling the well to be cleaned out easily. Fix with screws driven upwards through the end rails and with recessed screws passed downwards through the top into the apron piece.

A stop is fitted as shown in Fig. 4.6. It is simply a
block of about 38 mm by 25 mm passed tightly through a
hole in the top. A bolt passed through the leg engages
with a slot in the stop, this allowing the stop to be moved
up or down. A wing nut tightened over a washer holds the
stop in any desired position.

Vice fitting depends on the particular make. It involves
cutting away the front of the bench, and in all probability
a packing piece will be needed beneath. Wood jaws must
be fitted to the metal vice. Holes bored into the right-hand
leg take a peg to support long pieces held in the vice. The
drawer can be a plain box, either dovetailed or lap-jointed
together, with the bottom held in grooves or a slip moulding. Strips fixed to the sides at the top edges engage with
L-shaped runners fixed beneath the apron piece. At the
back, uprights can be dropped down from the back rail to
support the runners.

Cutting List

	Long cm	Wide cm	Thick mm
4 Legs	84	—	50 sq.
4 Rails	47	—	50 sq.
3 Rails	122	—	50 sq.
1 Apron	151	21	22
1 Top	151	29	38
1 Well bottom	151	31	6·5 ply
1 Back rail	151	6	22
1 Rack rail	151	7	13
2 Sloping ends	15	26	50
1 Shelf	130	47	6·5 ply
1 Drawer front	41	9	22
1 Drawer back	41	9	9·5
2 Drawer sides	41	9	9·5
1 Drawer bottom	40	9	6·5 ply
1 Stop	31	3·8	25

Fig. 4.7 An attractive greenhouse, 306 cm by 214 cm approx.

4.2 Span-roof Greenhouse, 306 cm by 214 cm approx.

This greenhouse could be enlarged or cut down to suit circumstances. Sizes are largely fixed by the pane width of the glass. This is 12 in, which enables a standard size

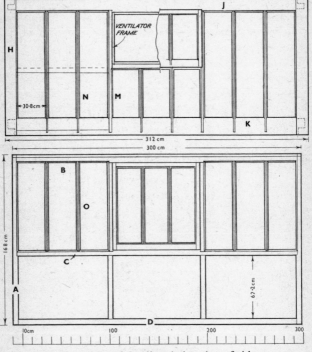

Fig 4.8 Roof detail and elevation of side

of glass to be cut economically. (At the time of going to press glass is still sold in Imperial sizes.) To take this the actual rebate clearance width is $12\frac{1}{8}$ in or 308 mm, so that there is an easy fit and allowance for a bed of putty.

It should be noted that metric timber may be slightly

smaller than Imperial sizes. Another point is that old stocks of Imperial sizes may still be sold. It is therefore necessary to fix dimensions according to the actual timber being used.

The whole thing is made up from two side frames, two end frames and the roofs. These are bolted together so that they can be taken apart. A concrete or brick footing is essential to keep the wood away from the ground, where it is liable to rot.

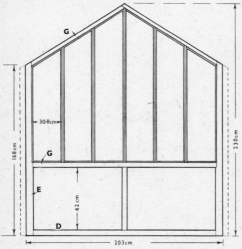

Fig. 4.9 Elevation of closed end

Make up the side frames as shown in Fig. 4.8. One can be fitted with a window hinged at the top and the other left plain or also fitted with a window. Details of the sections of the various main framework parts are shown in Fig. 4.11, from which it will be seen that the rebates for the glass are required in some portions but not all through. Joints are needed as in Fig. 4.12, and it will be seen that complications are avoided by cutting mitres on the laps formed by the rebates. Remember that the shoulder length is therefore taken to the rebates on such parts. As the rebate is 12·5 mm throughout, the shoulder length of top (*B*) and middle (*C*) rails is 25 mm longer than that of the bottom rail (*D*).

Mark out the mortise positions on the uprights (*A*) and gauge in where the rebates are to be worked. The mor-

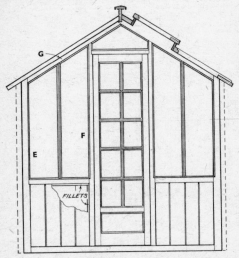

Fig. 4.10 Door end elevation

tises can either be taken right through and the tenons wedged at the outside, or they can be blind, in which case the joints should be pegged. Through mortising is rather stronger, but it leaves the tenon ends exposed—always a weakness, in that end grain is where rot begins and the wedges are liable to drop out in time, again allowing moisture to penetrate.

To enable the stopped rebates to be worked chop a short portion with the chisel right up to the stop. The main part of the rebate can then be worked with the rebate plane. Saw the tenons and cut the shoulders and mitres. The top rail (*B*) has to be bevelled at the top to agree with the slope of the roof, and this can be done

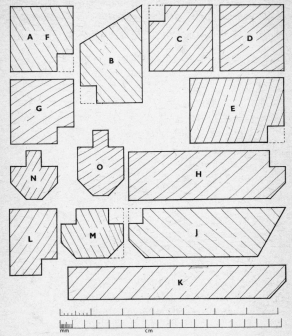

Fig. 4.11 Sections of various members with scales

before assembling. If a circular saw is available, this is the easiest way of cutting.

End frames are shown in Figs. 4.9 and 4.10, and it will be seen that construction is similar but that the sloping top members are fitted with open mortise and tenon joints, as shown in Fig. 4.13. Here it is advisable to use an adjustable sliding bevel to mark the joint or nail two

pieces of wood together at the required angle for marking. At the apex an open mortise and tenon joint is used
again.

Mortise positions for the bars can be marked in, noting
that they will have to slope at an angle on the sloping
members (*G*, Fig. 4.13). For the shoulder length of the

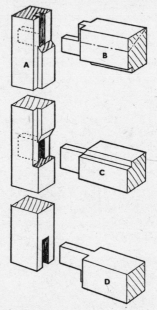

Fig. 4.12 Joints used in side framework

bars, however, it is advisable to put the main structure
together temporarily to enable exact measurements to be
taken. Standard bar stuff already rebated and moulded
or chamfered can be obtained. All frames should be
assembled with either resin glue or thick paint. If the
latter is used, the joints should be pegged if they are not
being wedged. Test each frame for squareness when

assembling, and nail a batten across temporarily to hold the whole until the glue has set.

When erecting the structure, fix one side to an end with two cramps, make sure that they are level and bore bolt holes as in Fig. 4.15. Carriage bolts should be used, and the nuts should be tightened over washers. Having fixed the whole, the tops of the uprights can be sawn to agree with the slope of the roofs. All raw, exposed wood should

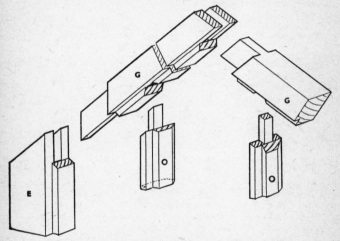

Fig. 4.13 Joints used in sloping members of end

be given a coat of priming. In fact, the frames should not be assembled until the roof frames are ready, but we deal with the assembling now for convenience. The lower portion is filled in with match boarding or weather boards, this being nailed to fillets fixed round as in Fig. 4.10.

Fig. 4.8 shows the roof frame and Fig. 4.14 gives the joints required. Note that, although the top rail (*J*) is of the same thickness as the sides (*H*), the bottom rail (*K*) is thinner, so that the glass rests on it and water is thus free

Cutting List

		Long cm	Wide cm	Thick mm
Side frames				
A	4 Uprights	172	—	50 sq.
B	2 Rails	301	7·5	50
C, D	4 Rails	301	—	50 sq.
	4 Uprights	76	—	50 sq.
	4 Uprights	102	—	50 sq.
O	8 Bars	100	—	—
O	4 Bars	91	—	—
	36 Matchings	64	15	19
	(or use horizontal weather boarding)			
	4 Window rails	94	—	50 sq.
	4 Stiles	94	—	50 sq.
End frames				
E	4 Uprights	172	7·5	50
F	2 Uprights	220	—	50 sq.
	1 Upright	75	—	50 sq.
G	1 Rail	205	—	50 sq.
G	2 Rails	80	—	50 sq.
D	2 Rails	205	—	50 sq.
G	4 Rails	130	—	50 sq.
G	1 Rail	69	—	50 sq.
O	1 Bar	168	—	—
O	2 Bars	145	—	—
O	4 Bars	122	—	—
	20 Matchings	64	15	19
	2 Stiles	196	7·5	38
	2 Rails	59	10	38
	1 Rail	59	15	38
N	1 Bar	160	—	—
N	4 Bars	58	—	—
Roof				
J	2 Rails	312	13	38
K	2 Rails	312	18	22
H	4 Stiles	150	13	38
M	4 Stiles	135	5	38
	2 Rails	100	5	38
N	8 Bars	130	—	—
N	4 Bars	70	—	—

Cutting List (cont.)

		Long cm	Wide cm	Thick mm
	Roof (cont.)			
	4 Frame rails	100	9	22
	4 Frame rails	56	9	22
	4 Stiles	63	5	38
	2 Rails	102	5	38
	2 Rails	102	8	22
N	4 Bars	60	—	—
	1 Ridge	322	12·5	22
	1 Capping	322	12·5	22

Allowance has been made in lengths and widths. Thicknesses are net. Small parts are extra.

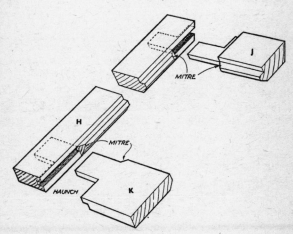

Fig. 4.14 Roof joints

Note that glass rests on bottom rail (*K*).

to drain off. Work rebates in the required positions. Two stout rails (*M*) are required to stiffen the centre and to give a fixing for the ventilator frame. Either both roofs or only one roof can have a ventilator.

In the best work tapering grooves are cut across the rail between each bar; these allow any condensation from the roof to drain away to the outside. They are not essential, however, and in their absence the water will merely run or drip down the side frames, where in the long run it will cause discoloration. The ventilator is made similarly to the main frame so that water is free to drain away at the lower edge without being trapped by a rebate.

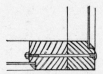

Fig. 4.15 How frames are bolted together

At the top a ridge piece is fitted and the roofs are bevelled to fit close up to this. At the ends the ridge piece is notched to fit over the end frames. To fix the roofs bolt through to the end frames and nail into the ridge piece. Finally, fit a capping over the latter. Drip grooves are worked at the edges to prevent water from seeping inwards. The door can be as in Fig. 4.9, or it can be of any standard pattern.

Before glazing it is essential that all surfaces, including the rebates, are given a coat of priming. The glass is then bedded in putty, an overlap being arranged as shown if necessary. When giving the undercoat and gloss coats, carry the paint slightly over onto the glass so that the whole is sealed.

4.3 Garden Seat, 120 cm long

When making a garden seat, the seat should be well below the height of an ordinary dining-room chair so that the legs of the sitter are comfortably rested. In determining the height, allow also for the likelihood of a cushion being

Fig. 4.16 Comfortable garden seat, 120 cm long

Could be in hardwood finished with varnish, or paint could be used to finish it.

used. It is also advisable to have an ample distance from front of seat to back. With a wide and fairly low seat, it is not necessary to give much of a rake to the back legs.

In Fig. 4.17 the seat rails (*D*) are shown as perfectly horizontal—the most simple in construction. If preferred, they may be arranged to slope gently towards the back—say, a matter of 12 mm. Alternatively, the top edges of the three seat rails may be slightly curved (concave) so that, when the laths are fitted, the seat has a dip of about 12 mm in the centre.

For a seat up to 120 cm long, follow the widths and thicknesses given in the cutting list. For a length of 140

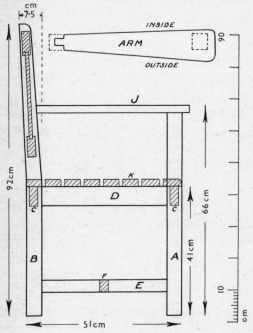

Fig. 4.17 Sectional end view showing rake of back

cm, increase the stuff for legs to 63 mm square, and use 75 mm by 38 mm for the seat rails and 50 mm by 38 mm for the underframing rails. This applies to hardwood. Note that animal glue is not used in the construction. All the joints are fitted with synthetic resin glue and secured with hardwood dowel pegs.

First complete the two ends. The back legs (*B*) can be got out of boards 75 mm wide to allow for the rake. At the top they may be tapered slightly (not more than 6 mm), as indicated in Fig. 4.17. The rails (*D*) and (*E*) are tenoned to the legs. The arm (*J*) enters the back leg by a tenon. It should be wedge-pegged to the front leg through

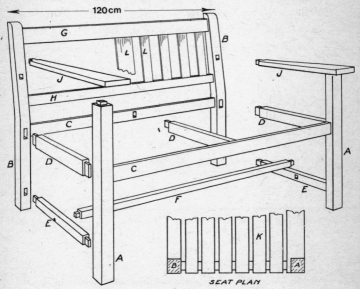

Fig. 4.18 How the seat is assembled

the stub tenon shown in Fig. 4.18. Note the plan of arm in Fig. 4.17.

The upper back (Fig. 4.18) is next tackled. The rails (*G*) and (*H*) are grooved 15 mm wide and about 9 mm deep throughout their length to take the splats (*L*), which, correctly spaced, are glued in. Short lengths of hardwood (9 mm by 15 mm) are cut to fit the spaces left in the grooves between the splats and also painted in. The seat may now be assembled, the two completed ends being connected by the seat rails (*C, C*), the back (*G, H*) and the stretcher rail (*F*), all tenoned in and well cramped. Do not overlook the intermediate cross rail (*D*), which is required as a central support for the seat laths (*K*). In screwing down these laths use brass screws, carefully countersinking for the heads and driving them well home. Also note that the laths overhang the rails at the ends, being kept flush in line with the legs.

Cutting List

		Long cm	Wide cm	Thick mm
A	2 Front legs	67	—	50 sq.
B	2 Back legs	93	7·5	50
C	2 Seat rails	120	6·3	32
D	3 Seat rails	51	6·3	32
E	2 Underframe rails	50	3·8	32
F	1 Stretcher rail	119	3·8	32
G	1 Back rail	120	7·5	32
H	1 Lower back rail	120	6·5	32
J	2 Arms	54	10	25
K	7 Seat laths	120	5	22
	1 Front lath	120	6·5	22
L	8 Back splats	28	5	15
	1 Middle splat	28	13	15

Working allowance has been made in lengths and widths. Thicknesses are net.

4.4 Timber-framed Asbestos-Cement Garage

Car owners can save quite a lot of the expense of a garage by building their own. That shown in Fig. 4.19 measures about 488 cm by 275 cm, with an effective clearance width between the doors of 220 cm. (If necessary these sizes could be adapted within a little to suit special requirements.) It has flat asbestos-cement panels at the

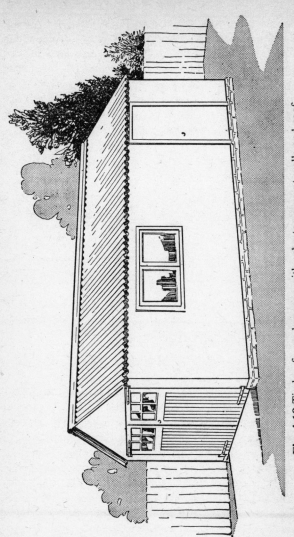

Fig. 4.19 Timber-framed garage with asbestos-cement walls and roof

sides and a corrugated asbestos-cement roof. The framing is of timber, and before a start is made the requirements of the local authorities should be ascertained because some object to timber.

It will be seen from Fig. 4.20 that the front and rear frames are contained between the sides to which they are bolted. Trusses are built at the top, and it should be noted that special angle braces are fitted at the top corners of

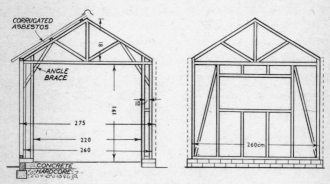

Fig. 4.20 Elevations of ends

All sizes are in centimetres.

the front. These are fixed behind the frames, and their purpose is to stop side racking. They are unnecessary at the back because there is a sufficient rigidity. Of the sides (Fig. 4.21), one has a window and a door; the other can have a window only or be blank. A centre truss is added, as shown in Fig. 4.22, and purlins are fixed along the whole to which the corrugated asbestos can be bolted.

The whole thing should rest on a brick footing laid on concrete foundation. A suitable mix for the latter is 5 parts shingle, 3 parts sand and 1 part Portland cement. This is laid in a channel dug round beneath the walls, and three courses of bricks are put on top at sides and back, and at the immediate returns at the front. Between these footings the earth is excavated and a layer of hard core put down. On this is a 10-cm concrete surface, and it is a good plan to give a slight slope towards the front so that

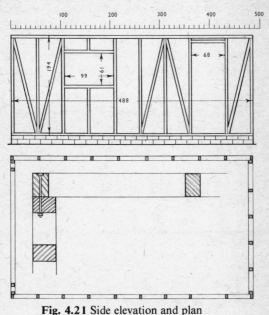

Fig. 4.21 Side elevation and plan

All sizes are in centimetres.

water, whether from a wet car or when draining the car radiator, passes out beneath the doors easily.

The frames are put together with simple halved or notched joints. One good plan is to halve the main corners and notch the others. Remember to allow for the side door and window, and add diagonal braces wherever practicable. The simplest plan is to assemble each frame on flat ground. Test for squareness and insert the braces, skew-nailing where necessary. In the case of the front frame, make sure that the lower end is exactly the same width as the top. A good plan is to nail a batten across temporarily. It is as well to bolt the angle braces, as they take considerable strain. The fact that they pass across the corners does not matter because there is ample clearance for the car.

To erect the whole put two adjacent frames together, holding with a cramp, and bore to take three 8-mm bolts

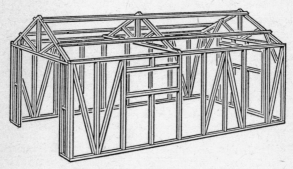

Fig. 4.22 General construction

at each corner. Work round the whole in the same way. It will be seen from Fig. 4.20 that the frames are level with the *outside* of the brick footing or project slightly, so that the asbestos-cement panels can pass down slightly and thus prevent water from getting in. In any case, it is as well to put a strip of damp-course felt beneath the framework as a safeguard against damp creeping up.

The centre roof truss is made up as a separate unit, and, as it is desirable for it to rest on the side frames, the rafters must be set in slightly so that they are in alignment with front and back. The exact position is easily found by placing the bottom tie beam immediately behind front or back, and cutting and fitting the rafters so that they line up with those of front and back. Nail in position and add the two purlins at each side. Note that they allow the roofing asbestos-cement to rest also upon the top rails of the side frames (see Fig. 4.20).

The covering now follows. The roofing is held with galvanised screws, the heads of which bear onto specially curved washers. The holes to take them must be drilled through the hills of the corrugations, not the valleys, and the heads of the bolts should be smeared with mastic to keep out water. A galvanised ridge strip is added lastly, as in Fig. 4.20.

Side covering should be fixed with galvanised roundhead screws tightened over washers. Where joining is necessary, a strip of wood can be placed over the joint. Incidentally, it is a good plan to ascertain the standard sizes of panel available and arrange the uprights of the frames accordingly, so that joints can occur in the middle of the uprights. In any case, it is as well to add wood corner strips as a protection since the asbestos-cement is somewhat brittle.

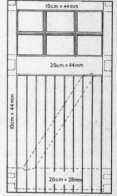

Fig. 4.23 Details of doors

Doors are made as in Fig. 4.23. The rails are through-tenoned and wedged, and a brace is added to each, as shown by the dotted lines. Note that top and middle rails are 44 mm thick but that at the bottom is only 28 mm. This allows 16-mm matching to pass right down to the bottom. Standard section bars are used for the glazed top portion, the glass being bedded in putty and a putty seam put round inside. It is usual to use frosted glass. Special stout garage door hinges are used.

Casement windows can be used at the side and back. Standard sash material is used and the usual through tenons cut, these being wedged at the outside. To keep out damp a fillet is nailed round the frame immediately behind the window, this forming a rebate. For the small side door, either a panelled or a ledged-and-braced type can be made. Here again, a fillet at the inside helps to keep out moisture.

All woodwork can have the usual three-coat finish, but it is advisable to give the asbestos-cement panels a special sealing coat before painting.

4.5 Double Coal Bunker

Exact sizes of the bunker can be varied to suit the space available and the accommodation needed. As shown, it will hold in the region of a ton of fuel, though if the latter is light and bulky it will not hold so much. Except for the concrete base, the whole thing is of timber, consisting of separate frames of 5 cm by 5 cm deal, put together with simple notched joints nailed together and covered with boards either tongued together or of weathered section. It is intended that the sides be painted and the roof covered with roofing felt. The lids are loose and have simply to be lifted off when the bunker is being filled. Access to the hatches is by means of sliding doors, which are raised.

The concrete base should be about 10 cm thick and should be laid on a flat surface that has been consolidated by tamping. Loose earth is liable to sink, so that the concrete has unequal support and is thus liable to crack. The mix should be 1 cement, 3 sand, 3 broken stone and just over $\frac{1}{2}$ water. Mix the materials dry, turning them over three times, then add the water, using a watering can. An edging of boards held in place with pegs driven into the ground should be prepared to contain the concrete. The top edges should be made true to enable the surface to be levelled by drawing a straight-edge back and forth across them.

Back and front frames are rectangular and are made to the sizes given in Fig. 4.25. It will be realised that the top edges of both have to be bevelled to allow for the sloping roof, but this is best done after the parts are together. So far as the top and bottom rails are concerned, all are

Fig. 4.24 Double coal bunker in wood on concrete base

identical except the bottom front, which is in three pieces to allow for the hatches. Set out one and mark the others from it. Notches 6 mm deep are cut, the idea being that these resist all movement, the nails merely serving to keep the parts in position. The uprights are in two sizes for the back, those at the ends and those between the rails. If the former are cut out and marked first, the length of the others can be taken from the notch shoulders, with 12 mm added to allow the projection into the notches. For the front, three lengths of uprights are needed: those at the ends, those at each side of the hatch and the middle ones

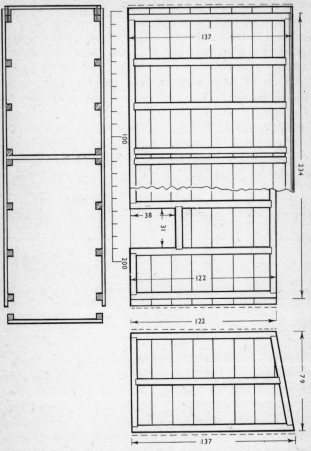

Fig. 4.25 Sizes and construction of the four frames, and plan view showing how parts are bolted together

All sizes are in centimetres.

where the partition is fixed. Here again, the easiest plan is to mark the end ones and mark the others from them. Note that notches are needed in the hatch uprights.

Fix all the parts together with French nails and test for squareness. A batten nailed diagonally across will hold the whole true temporarily until the boarding is added.

The ends are slightly more complicated, in that the sloping top rail has to be allowed for. The simplest way is to fix the bottom rail to the uprights, leaving the latter 25 mm or so long, and nail a temporary batten across all

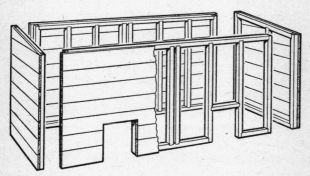

Fig. 4.26 Exploded view showing frames and how they are boarded

three, making sure that all are the same distance apart when measured across horizontally. The top rail can then be placed in position and pencil lines drawn in to show the amount to be sawn off; also the angle. Again nail and test for squareness, nailing a diagonal across when true.

When fixing the boarding at the ends, the edges are finished flush. At front and back, however, the boarding projects so that it covers over the framework of the ends. Use two nails through the boarding into each framework member and 'dovetail' the nails so that they have maximum grip. The partition can simply be a series of rough

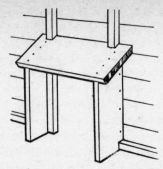

Fig. 4.27 Inside guard which keeps the opening clear

boards contained between the centre uprights. It is best added after the main frames have been assembled. To hold the sides together use three 8-mm or 10-mm carriage bolts at each corner, placing washers beneath the nuts so that they do not bite into the wood. The gaps at the corners are filled in with 22-mm fillets nailed in.

Fig. 4.27 shows how a guard is fixed inside each hatch so that the fuel is kept as far back as possible. The parts are nailed together and to the framework. The roof con-

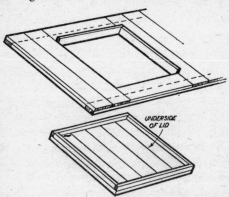

UNDERSIDE OF LID

Fig. 4.28 Details of top and lids covering filling apertures

sists of a series of boards running from front to back, with a strip along the length at top and bottom at the underside, as shown in Fig. 4.28. Filling-in pieces are added at the ends. To raise the lids a lining to project about 25 mm is nailed around the openings. The lids themselves have an edging at the underside to make a generous fit over the lining. After painting, the whole roof and lids are covered with roofing felt.

Hatch doors are made to slide in grooves worked in uprights fixed at each side of the opening. The tops of these uprights are cut at an angle so that a top can be added to throw off water. A simple hardwood turnbuckle holds the door in the raised position when required.

4.6 Garden Frame

A frame can be of practically any size. That shown in Fig. 4.29 is about 120 cm by 90 cm. It consists in the main of a front, back and two sides, the latter being lower

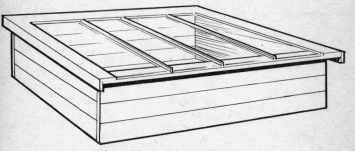

Fig. 4.29 Simple garden frame

at the front to enable water to drain away easily at the top. Match boarding 22 mm thick is suitable to use, and it is held together with cross-battens nailed on at the ends. One point to note is that the top piece of matching is

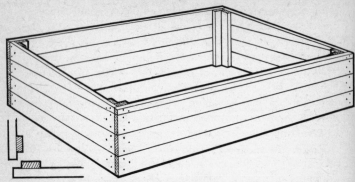

Fig. 4.30 How the main framework is made

necessarily tapered, and it is advisable to avoid making
this run to a point at the front because it would be
awkward to nail. Leave it at least 50 mm wide. It will be
seen from Fig. 4.30 that the cross-battens stand in from
the end in every case. This makes a much stronger joint
when the whole thing is assembled.

To make a really good job of the top frame it should be
put together with mortise and tenon joints wedged from
outside and held with paint. A simple alternative is given
in Fig. 4.31. The main frame is of 32-mm stuff, and

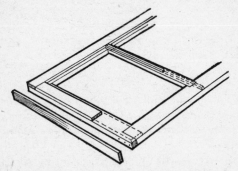

Fig. 4.31 Construction of the top light

notches are cut at the ends of the sides to enable it to be
nailed up strongly. In a similar way, the intermediate
cross rails are fixed in notches. To form a rebate for the
glass 12-mm strips are fixed to the top at back and sides.
These are 12 mm narrower than the main frame. They
are nailed down, a coat of paint being brushed on first.
(Glue, of course, is useless.) There is no strip at the front
because the glass reaches right over the front rail, thus
allowing water to drain off freely. Either single sheets of
glass can be used, or two or more panes to each space. In
the latter case the bottom glass is laid in position first, the
second overlapping it by about 50 mm. In any case a
good bed of putty should be laid in the rebate first and the
glass pressed down. Remember to paint the rebate first
or the putty will not adhere. Side strips can be added
as in Fig. 4.31, and also one at the back. The latter
prevents water from trickling through into the inside of
the frame.

The whole thing should be well painted or creosoted to
keep out the damp.

4.7 Garden Workshed

Those who can spare the space for the purpose will find a
garden workshop a tremendous asset. It saves the inevitable dust and dirt from being trodden into the house, and,
being isolated, the noise will not disturb others. That
shown in Fig. 4.32 is of the simple lean-to type which can
stand in practically any position, and it is portable in that
it is made in six separate sections bolted together. This
facilitates its easy removal to another site if desired. The
side and end windows give ample light, and the door at
one end enables timber, etc., to be carried in or out easily.
As given in Fig. 4.33, it measures about 300 cm by 180
cm. This is really the smallest practicable size for a

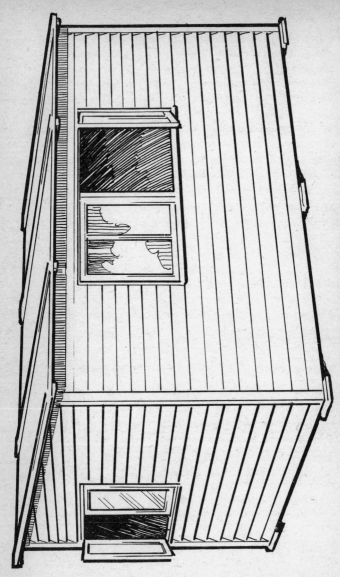

Fig. 4.32 Useful garden workshop made to take to pieces

workshop, and 30 cm or so could easily be added without seriously altering the construction.

Weather boarding is suggested for the covering shown in Fig. 4.36. This looks attractive in a garden, though tongued and grooved boards could be substituted if desired, in which case the boards should be upright rather than horizontal. One point to note in this connection is

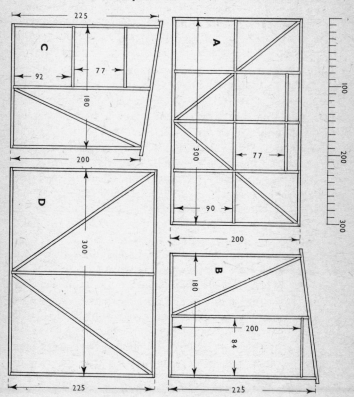

Fig. 4.33 Elevations with sizes of the main frames

All sizes are in centimetres.

that a saving in labour can often be effected by fixing the dimensions in accordance with the material being used. For instance, if the weather boarding is 15 cm wide exclusive of the overlap, it is an advantage to make the height of back and front multiples of 15, so that unnecessary work in ripping down timber is avoided. The same thing applies to the door, the width of which is controlled by the width of matching being used. The floor boarding, too, can be made to fit the width. Another point worth bearing in mind is that the window sashes can, if preferred, be obtained ready-made. They usually run in standard sizes, and it is as well to ascertain what these are before beginning the work so that the positions of the members of the framework can be decided to suit.

Begin work on the front and back frames, making these out of 50 mm by 50 mm stuff. The joints are of the simplest notched variety, put together with nails driven in askew. Assemble the parts on a flat patch of ground and test for squareness. Temporary laths can be nailed across the whole to steady them. The addition of the diagonal struts makes them perfectly stiff. The end frames follow, and it will be seen that they are higher than the front and rear by the thickness of the rafters (50 mm).

The floor is made to the overall size of the shed when assembled, since the frames stand on it. A framework is made of 100-mm by 50-mm joists. There are the four pieces forming the sides and a series of intermediate ones running lengthwise. They are joined with either mortise and tenon or notched joints, and the whole is nailed together. This framework (forming the joists) can be seen in Fig. 4.34. The whole thing rests on brick foundations built on concrete. There is one at each corner and one in the middle of each long side. The frame rests on these, any levelling being done by packing in pieces of slate. The flooring is of 22-mm stuff nailed down.

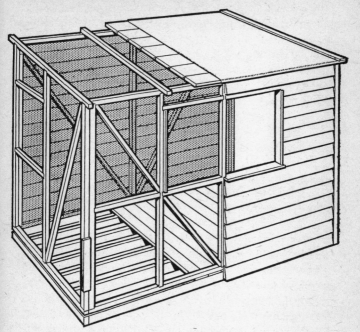

Fig. 4.34 Cut-away view showing general construction

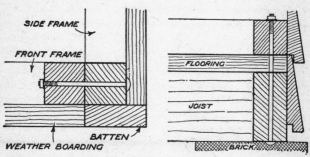

Fig. 4.35 Plan section through corner

Fig. 4.36 Section through base

The frames are erected on this floor and held with bolts. The simplest method of erection is to hold one side in position by nailing to it a couple of struts to rest on the ground. Place one adjacent side against it and fix the two together with a couple of handscrews or cramps. Bolt holes can then be bored through the two whilst they are together, thus ensuring their being in alignment. Use 10-

Fig. 4.37 Plan section through window

mm bolts, but make the holes full in size so that there is a certain amount of latitude. When the two are together, they will support each other and the remaining two can be added. Fig. 4.35 is a section through one corner and shows the bolts. The whole thing is held down onto the flooring with bolts, and the holes for these are bored after the frames are in position. Boring the holes through the two ensures alignment. Do not put the holes at the corners, as the bit would foul the brick foundations.

Fig. 4.38 Details of door

The door and window linings follow. Fig. 4.37 is a section through the window. If the frames are being made, lengths of 38-mm square stuff can be put together with halved joints. Wider battens are then fitted to the inside to form a rebate for the glass. The outer pieces are butted together. This method is not so strong as the mortise and tenon joint,

but it is a reasonable substitute for a cheap job. The
boarding is straightforward. Each boarding finishes off
level with the framework to which it is fixed, and a batten
is nailed in the corner as in Fig. 4.35. This covers the end
grain.

The roof consists of four to six purlins or sloping rails
of 50 mm by 50 mm stuff covered with 19 mm matching.
It is held down with bolts and is covered with roofing felt
fixed with clout nails. 50-mm by 6-mm strips are nailed
on top through to the rafters to hold it.

All woodwork should be either painted or creosoted as
a protection against weather.

*   *   *

*Garden carpentry may be rougher than cabinet work, but
that doesn't mean that you can be careless.*

*   *   *

*If a shed roof leaks, put it right straightway. Otherwise
you will have something else to put right as well.*

*   *   *

*Paint your outdoor woodwork periodically; it will last
twice as long.*

*   *   *

*Nails are invaluable in carpentry, but remember that they
do not take the place of a joint.*

5 Small Items to Make

5.1 Small Boxes

Boxes of the kind shown in Figs. 5.1 and 5.3 could be used for cards, trinkets, cigarettes or general oddments. The sizes given could be adapted to individual requirements, but it should be remembered that interior sizes should be adapted to the particular purpose for which the box is intended. That shown in Fig. 5.1 would look well

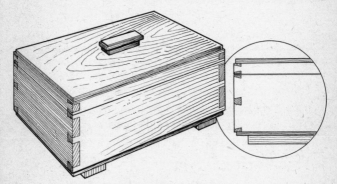

Fig. 5.1 Small box in oak. Design *A*

in solid oak. Veneers are used in the box illustrated in Fig. 5.3, and a combination of straight-grained woods and an attractive burr would look well.

5.1.1 *Design A*

For the box in Fig. 5.1, cut out the sides and ends, the length to the finished size and the width to include the lid, with a small allowance for the saw-cut made when the lid portion is sawn away. Space out the dovetails on the sides as shown in Fig. 5.2, noting that a single small dovetail is

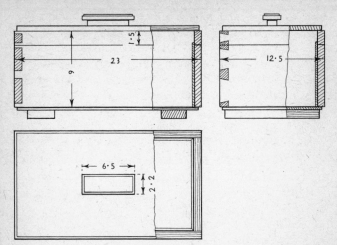

Fig. 5.2 Elevations and plan of box illustrated in Fig. 5.1
(Design *A*)

All sizes are in centimetres.

allowed on the lid. Cut the joints and, when satisfactory, glue the whole together. When set, level the joints and clean up the sides. Run a gauge round where the lid is to be separated and saw away as in Fig. 5.5. Plane the edges

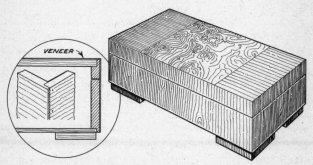

Fig. 5.3 Small veneered box. Design *B*

to a neat finish and add the bottom. A lining fitted to the box should stand up slightly at the top, as shown in Fig. 5.6, so that the lid is held in position. Lining corners are mitred, and if cut to a fairly tight fit there is no need to glue in position. The lid is glued to its framing and stands in all round. A handle is made from two pieces glued together and screwed in position from beneath. Wax gives a good finish, but it helps to give a thin preliminary coat of plastic lacquer as it builds up a slight gloss and helps to keep out dirt.

Cutting List

	Long cm	Wide cm	Thick mm
2 Sides	24	9·5	9·5
2 Ends	13	9·5	9·5
1 Top	23	12·5	6·5
1 Bottom	23	12·5	3·2
2 Feet	12·5	3·6	9·5
1 Handle	7	2·2	6·5
1 Handle	6·5	1·3	6·5
2 Linings	22	8·5	3·2
2 Linings	11·5	8·5	3·2

5.1.2 *Design B*

The general procedure for this box is similar to that for box *A*, but the corners are put together with lapped joints rather than with dovetails. The sides are trimmed to the overall length, but the ends are less than the finished size by the thickness of the laps, as shown in Fig. 5.4. Both lid and bottom fit in rebates, and this rebating must be done before assembling. The parts are glued and pinned together, and the lid is separated later as shown in Fig. 5.5. Remember not to put any nails where the saw-cut has to be made. If the parts are veneered before separation, there will necessarily be good grain match all

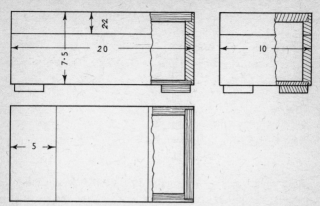

Fig. 5.4 Elevations and plan of veneered box illustrated in Fig. 5.3 (Design *B*)

All sizes are in centimetres.

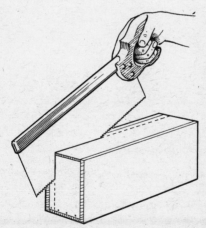

Fig. 5.5 How lid of box is separated by sawing

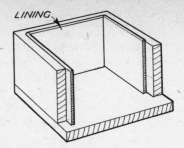

Fig. 5.6 How lining is added to box

If a tight fit is made, no fixing is necessary.

round. In this case the sawing line should be cut round with the cutting gauge. The simplest way of veneering is to use the caul method. The lid can either be hinged or the box can be fitted with a lining to keep it in position. The feet are glued and pinned underneath.

Cutting List

	Long cm	Wide cm	Thick mm
2 Sides	21	8	9·5
2 Ends	10·5	8	9·5
1 Top	20	10	9·5
1 Bottom	20	10	5
4 Feet	4	4	6·5

5.2 Modern-style Plate Rack

This type of rack is vastly more convenient than the old square kind with vertical bars through which plates had to be passed. The bars are at the back and shelves only; this makes the rack much more convenient to use and easily cleaned. Only the ends are painted, the rails and bars being left in the white.

For the ends, use either block board or multi-ply 12·5 mm thick. Set out the shape of one to the sizes in Fig. 5.8 and cut out. The interior piercings can be sawn with a coping saw or bow saw, holes being first bored at the corners to enable the saw to be started. Incidentally, the holes make nice rounded corners. The six rails are 25-mm squares planed to octagonal shape and are jointed to the ends with mortise and tenon joints. They should preferably be in teak. It makes a stronger job if the tenons

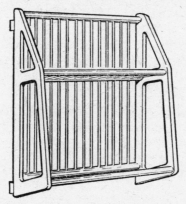

Fig. 5.7 Modern-style plate rack

are taken right through and are wedged at the outside. Cut the mortises and pencil–round all the outer edges of the ends.

Prepare the rails to square section and mark the tenons at the ends. Holes to take the 9·5-mm dowels are needed, and obviously these must all be in alignment. The best way is to step out the required number on one rail, using dividers. A certain amount of trial-and-error stepping is required. When satisfactory, cramp all six rails together with the shoulders exactly level and square the dowel marks across all. A marking gauge set to the centre of the

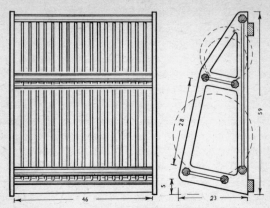

Fig. 5.8 Elevations of plate rack with sizes

All sizes are in centimetres.

wood is used to cut each line. Since many holes have to be bored, and because it is essential that they are all the same depth, it is advisable to use a depth gauge on the bit. When all are completed, plane off the corners of the rails so that the octagonal shape is formed. It makes a more

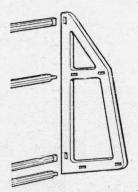

Fig. 5.9 How rails are joined to ends

durable job if the bars are in teak. As dowels in this wood are difficult to obtain, an alternative is to have square bars, cutting these from teak and fitting them into square mortises.

The whole is now ready to assemble. There is no need to glue the bars, but the tenons must, of course, be glued. Put the back and shelves together independently (all the sets of dowels must clearly be to the same length) and add the ends, gluing the tenons. Cramp if possible and knock in wedges at the outside. The cramps must be clear of the rails, as otherwise it would be impossible to drive in the wedges. When the glue has set, the tenons can be levelled at the ends and the two back rails screwed on. These are useful, not only for fixing to the wall but also to bring the whole forward, thus giving clearance for the plates (see Fig. 5.8).

Cutting List

	Long cm	Wide cm	Thick mm
2 Ends	60	24	12·5
6 Rails	49	—	25 sq.
2 Rails	49	5	19
17 Dowels	47	—	9·5
17 Dowels	15	—	9·5
17 Dowels	11	—	9·5

5.3 Folding Ironing-table

To make it sound, a good solid top board (*A*, Fig. 5.11) of 19 mm or 22 mm is required, one end being pointed as shown and the edges gently rounded, for the table illustrated in Fig. 5.10. At the square end (where the iron may rest) the board is covered with a sheet of asbestos, held down by 9·5 mm by 6·5 mm strips (*B*, Fig. 5.11).

The board is otherwise covered first with a piece of old
blanket and later with a piece of calico. The material is
strained to fold over the edges and is neatly tacked,
preferably with brass-headed nails.

The folding stand calls for two frames, one 117 cm or
120 cm long, the other 90 cm long. The shorter frame is
adjusted in width so that, when pivoted with iron bolts, it
will fold within the legs of the longer frame. The sizes

Fig. 5.10 Simple folding ironing-table

may be taken from the scale but must be carefully tested
in the actual making. The legs (*C* and *E*) may be of 38
mm by 22 mm strips, whilst the cross-bracing laths (*D*)
and (*F*) may be 16 mm by 9·5 mm, the strips being
halved where they cross. The strips should be of hardwood.

The longer outer frame has a pair of small iron angle-
brackets pivot-screwed to the inner faces of the legs at the
top, these brackets being screwed later to the batten (*K*)
under the top board. The shorter inner frame has a top
rail (*G*) let into the legs and screwed. The exact point for

pivoting the frames must be determined when assembling. The reader will find it of great help to make a working drawing of the elevation (see Fig. 5.11) to half size. When the height to table-top (say, 86 cm) has been determined,

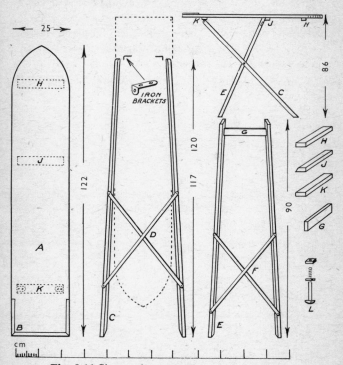

Fig. 5.11 Sizes and construction of ironing-table

he may then take two thin laths of the required length, lay these crosswise on the drawing and adjust them till he gets them in the right position. The point for the pivot bolts is then struck and the drawing can be completed. An important advantage of the drawing is that the correct bevels at the floor end of the legs and the bevel at the top of legs (*E*) may be marked.

K is the batten to which the folding stand is hinged by means of the iron brackets and should be of 22-mm hardwood. The batten (*J*) acts as a stop for the shorter frame. The third batten (*H*) is necessary to keep the top board out of winding but has no connection with the folding frames. To secure the top board when the article is in use it is well to screw a brass hook to the rail (*G*) of shorter frame, this to engage an eye screwed into the batten (*J*) against which the frame rests. The centre pivot bolts (*M*) may be 50 mm long by 6·5 mm diameter, each provided with a washer and nut.

Cutting List

		Long cm	Wide cm	Thick mm
A	Top board	123	25·5	19
B	Strip for top board	65	0·95	6·5
C	2 Legs	122	4	22
D	2 Strips	62	1·8	16
E	2 Legs	94	4	22
F	2 Strips	50	1·8	16
G	1 Rail	24	40	19
H, J, K	3 Battens	23	4	22

5.4 Table Lamp

This makes a useful bedside lamp. It is in modern style, consisting of a main stem which is rounded at the extreme top and bottom but resolves into a square section with rounded corners towards the middle. It is joined to the base with a short length of brass tube, which should be polished and lacquered. Practically any attractive hardwood can be used, but the base should be as heavy as possible. In fact, if a large shade is used, it is advisable to weight the base with lead, the underside having a recess cut in it and the lead inserted. To give a neat finish a piece of baize is afterwards glued over the whole.

To avoid the necessity of boring a hole right down the centre of the stem—always an awkward job—the latter is made in two pieces with a groove down the centre of each, and afterwards glued together. It is, of course, desirable for the grain of the two pieces to match as closely as possible so that the joint is unnoticeable. In fact, the ideal way is to have a piece of stuff just over 40 mm in section, rip it down the middle, groove the joining surfaces and rejoint. In this way the grain will obviously match. Whichever method is followed, prepare the two pieces, groove them and glue together. Now plane the whole to a square section, and at the two ends draw in a circle of the finished diameter. To do this at the top a small temporary plug is inserted to provide a centre in which the compasses or dividers

Fig. 5.12 Table lamp for the bedside

can be inserted. At the bottom the same thing applies, but a permanent plug has to be glued in because the bit that bores the tube hole has to be centred in it. It is, in fact, convenient to bore this hole before any shaping of the stem is started because, since the sides are straight and square, it is easier to judge whether the bit is being held in true alignment. It is obviously essential for the hole to be true, and a good plan is to cramp straight strips of wood on two adjacent sides and keep the bit in alignment with these when boring.

When working the shaping, begin by planing the four sides to a sweet curve, leaving the middle practically untouched but curving to meet the circles at the ends. Make sure that the curvature is the same on all four sides. This can be tested by holding the stem cornerwise to-

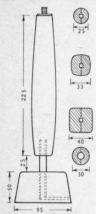

wards the eye, when the near corner will appear as a straight line if the curvature of the sides is equal. Follow by taking off the corners at 45 degrees, with just a slight bevel at the middle but increasing to the extent of the circles at the ends. Treat all four corners equally, and finish off by taking off the arrises so that these are pencil-rounded corners at the middle but with the square-ness gradually rounded over until the section is that of the circles at the ends. Finish with *middle 2* glasspaper followed by *No. 1*, finishing with *Flour* grade.

Fig. 5.13 Elevation with sizes and sections of stem

All sizes are in millimetres.

The base is prepared as a square block, and the sides then bevelled to a line gauged round the top surface. Finally, the corners are rounded. A centre hole is needed for the brass tube, and generally it will be convenient to bore this before bevelling the sides. In the best way an assistant will be able to indicate whether the brace is being held upright. He should stand at the side, because it is easy to detect whether the brace leans sideways but much more difficult to say whether it leans away from or towards the user. If this is not practicable, cramp the block to the bench, turn the brace a few revolutions, move the block through 90 degrees and turn the brace a few more times. In any case the centre should be squared round to the underside and the hole completed from beneath. A second hole to meet it is bored in the side to enable the flex to be threaded through. The brass tube is fixed in position with epoxy glue. It is advisable to file over the sharp corners at the bottom so that there is no danger of the insulation of the flex being cut. At the top a screw-on fitting is used to take the lampholder.

Cutting List

	Long cm	Wide cm	Thick mm
2 Stem pieces or	24	4·5	22
1 Piece	24	4·5	45
1 Base	10	10	52
1 Brass tube	10	—	9·5 diam.

5.5 Book Troughs

It is not essential to follow the sizes of the troughs illustrated in Figs. 5.14 and 5.16 exactly, but they can be taken as a general guide. That shown in Fig. 5.14 has two trough pieces fixed together at right angles and housed into two shaped ends, the whole assembled with glue, though the two pieces are also screwed together at the bottom. These two pieces can be cut out first and call for no special preparation beyond being planed accurately square. Obviously they must be exactly alike in length. Along the top edges slight chamfers are planed—no more than 3 mm wide. Having glued and screwed them together, a plane can be passed over the ends to level any

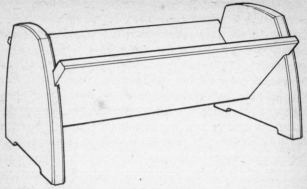

Fig. 5.14 Book rack or trough which would look well in oak

slight discrepancy. The joint between the two can also be levelled.

Cut out the two end pieces as squares of 16 cm. On them draw vertical centre lines on the inner faces and mark the sloping lines of the housing to receive the trough pieces, using a marking knife or chisel. To cut the housings it is advisable first to chop a square recess at

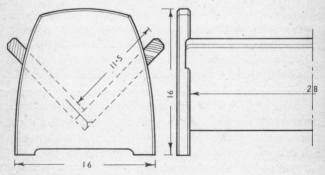

Fig. 5.15 Elevations of book rack shown in Fig. 5.14

All sizes are in centimetres.

the point where the two trough pieces meet. It should be about 6 mm deep. This recess enables the end of the back saw to emerge when sawing the sides of the housings, the saw being used in short strokes. Follow with the chisel down to nearly the finished depth and finish with the router, the latter ensuring an even depth throughout.

Either the coping saw or the bow saw can be used for cutting the shape of the ends. A cardboard templet of half the shape offers the simplest way of marking out, this being reversed about a centre line. Clean up the edges with the spokeshave and run a neat chamfer around both corners, as shown. Finally, the whole is glued together, cramps being used if possible. Clear lacquer can be used to finish the trough, or wax polish if preferred.

Cutting List

	Long cm	Wide cm	Thick mm
2 Ends	17	17	16
1 Trough piece	30	12	16
1 Trough piece	30	10·5	16

Fig. 5.16 gives a second design of trough which involves slightly more work but has no shaping to worry about. The base and the back rail are tenoned to pass right through the ends and are held with small wedges at the outside. Cut out the two ends to form rectangles 20 cm long by 16 cm wide, as shown by the dotted lines in Fig. 5.17. Mark on them the outer shaping; also the lines of the base and back rail. Note that these slope but are at right angles with each other. Since the mortises have to be cut right through, both sides must be marked.

When cutting the mortises, a centre hole should be bored in each, as this enables the waste to crumble away easily. Bore through from one side until the point of the

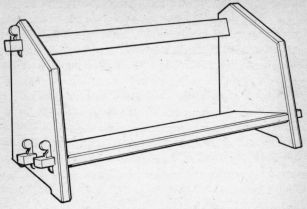

Fig. 5.16 Alternative design of rack

bit just emerges beneath and complete from the other side. The chisel is used to finish the mortises, care being taken to cut exactly to the line from each side. A point to note is that, since the mortises are cut to the full thickness of the base and rail, the mortise width must be taken from

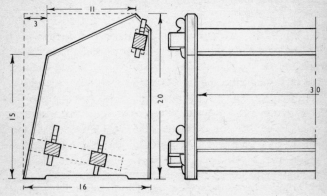

Fig. 5.17 Details of book rack shown in Fig. 5.16

All sizes are in centimetres.

this thickness. The jointing completed the outer shape can be sawn and the edges trimmed. Finally, a narrow chamfer is worked on both corners.

Both rail and base should be fixed together temporarily when marking the shoulder length. Saw the tenons to agree with the mortises and cut holes in them to receive the wedges. Since the purpose of the wedges is to exert a cramping as well as a retaining effect, these holes should stand slightly within the thickness of the ends. Unless this is done, the wedges will be ineffective. The outer edges of the holes, of course, must slope in alignment with the wedges. One advantage of this trough is that the parts can be polished separately before assembling, making for a clean finish.

Cutting List

	Long cm	Wide cm	Thick mm
2 Ends	21	17	17
1 Base	39	12·5	17
1 Rail	39	3·5	17

5.6 Tiled Tray

Two sizes of tray are shown in Fig. 5.19, these being intended to hold either six or fifteen tiles. A standard size of tile is still being made to Imperial measurements, $4\frac{1}{4}$ in square, the nearest metric equivalent being 108 mm, and we have therefore given two scales in Fig. 5.19. However, other sizes of tiles may be available and the overall dimensions of the tray should be made to suit the tiles actually being used.

Plywood 9·5 mm thick is used for the base, and this is cut larger than the combined size of the tiles by 30 mm in length and 24 mm in width, plus the joint allowance between the tiles. Many tiles have small distance lugs at the edges so that there is a small gap between them. It is as well in any case to cut the base slightly full to allow for any slight discrepancy in tile size and trim later.

The long edgings finish 12 mm wide by 10 mm thick, and the upper corners are slightly rounded. For the end handles, a section of 38 mm by 22 mm is needed, as shown by the dotted lines to the right, lower illustration, Fig. 5.19. In plan the outer edge is curved as shown, and

Fig. 5.18 Small tray with decorative tiles mounted on plywood

a wide chamfer is planed on the lower side. The upper side is rounded over. At the ends it will be found necessary to round over the chamfer to reduce the thickness, and, in fact, the corners of the plywood base will have to be slightly rounded to flow in with the curve. Having finished to an attractive shape, the whole is smoothed with glasspaper. Both handles and edgings are then polished. A suitable finish is plastic lacquer.

All these parts are held with screws driven upwards through the base. It is as well to hold the tiles loosely in position when doing this so that there is correct clearance. When satisfactory, the tiles are fixed with the

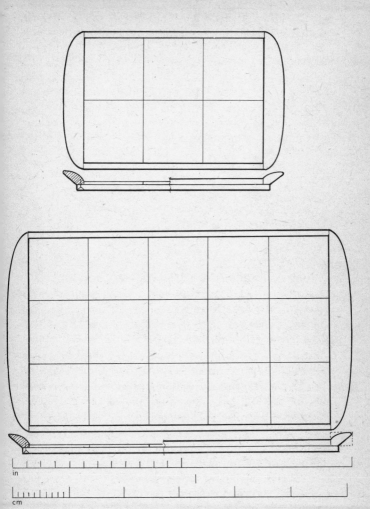

Fig. 5.19 Plans and elevations in part section of the two trays

special adhesive made for the purpose, and finally the joints between the tiles are filled with the white grouting preparation, again made for the purpose.

Cutting List

	Long cm	Wide cm	Thick mm
Small tray			
1 Base	36	25	9·5
2 Edgings	35	1·5	10
2 Handles	25	4	22
Large tray			
1 Base	60	35	9·5
2 Edgings	60	1·5	10
2 Handles	36	4	22

5.7 Spice Rack

This makes an attractive kitchen feature as well as being a useful item. It is intended to hold a dozen jars of spices, these jars being of decorative shape, each labelled with its contents. The rack itself is of light coloured pine, and would look well unstained and given a protective coat of clear lacquer. Alternatively, it could be painted to match any existing colour scheme. The design is reminiscent of the Austrian Tyrol, but if a simpler design is preferred the shaping of the ends could be omitted. It will be seen that the shelves are double-tenoned to fit through mortises cut in the ends and are wedged at the outside. Apart from making a strong structure, the method enables all the parts to be finished separately, this simplifying the process and making for a clean finish.

As the rack is quite small (the distance between the ends is only 30 cm), a standard size of softwood 7 cm by 10 mm is used. Since, however, this makes the shelves unnecessarily wide, it is cut down in width. The ends finish 6 cm wide and the shelves 5·6 cm, the latter allowing for a 4-mm back in either plywood or hardboard. The latter is suitable for a painted finish, but as

Fig. 5.20 Spice rack to hold twelve jars

plywood is of a lighter colour it would go better with lacquered pine.

Cut the shelves to finish 37·5 cm by 5·6 cm and the ends to 31 cm by 6 cm. Trim the ends of all parts on the shooting board. Fix the two ends together temporarily in the correct relation to each other, and square across the front edges the shelf positions. They are separated and the marks squared across both surfaces, the square being held with its butt against the face edge in all cases. The mortise gauge is set to the width of the chisel being used

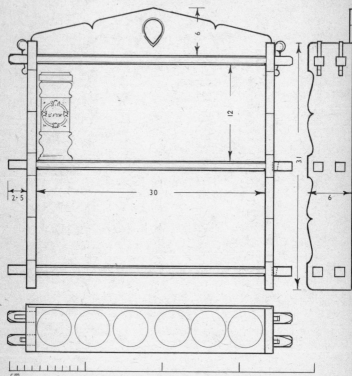

Fig. 5.21 Elevations and plan of spice rack
All sizes are in centimetres.

for mortising (10 mm or nearest Imperial equivalent) and used from the face edges. It should be realised that the tenons of the shelves have also to be marked out with the mortise gauge, and consequently the marking out of the shelves should be proceeded with so that both mortise and tenon at the front can be marked before the gauge is reset for the back mortise and tenon. Use the chisel or marking knife for marking the shoulders of the tenons, as this gives a definite line to which to cut.

In addition to the tenons, it is desirable at this stage also to mark the slots in which the wedges have to be

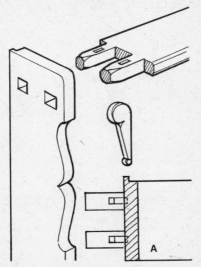

Fig. 5.22 How shelves are fitted to the ends

fitted. Note that the inner ends of the slots have to stand about 2 mm inside the outer surface of the ends, as shown at *A*, Fig. 5.22, because it is essential that the wedges bear against the ends. Unless this is done, the wedges will touch the ends of the slots and will not have any tightening effect. Owing to the wedge shape, the outer end of each slot will have to be cut at a corresponding angle. The ends of the tenons and the wedges can be given a decorative touch by bevelling after they have been fitted.

To receive the back the rear edges of the ends should be rebated (see plan Fig. 5.21). A templet of the shaping of the front edges should be cut for marking. The coping saw is used for cutting the shape, this being followed by the file and then by glasspaper wrapped around a rubber. Trim the back to size and cut the top to the decorative design shown. It fits behind the shelves and is screwed in position. Screw plates are used to fix the rack to the wall.

Cutting List

	Long cm	Wide cm	Thick mm
2 Ends	32	6·5	10
3 Shelves	38	6	10
1 Back	35	32	4 ply or hardboard
12 Wedges	5	1·5	5

6 Designs for Furniture

6.1 Oak Stool with Hinged Lid

The stool illustrated in Fig. 6.1 is Tudor Gothic in style and is designed specially for simplicity of construction. A useful box portion is arranged beneath the lid, and this should prove handy for oddments.

First prepare the two trestle ends or legs from 22-mm oak. They can be cut out first in the form of rectangles,

Fig. 6.1 Oak stool with hinged lid

33 cm by 25·5 cm. Having planed the edges square, the taper of the sides can be marked so that the top is 20 cm wide. The shape of the bottom can also be marked by drawing in the 2-cm squares and plotting the curves map-fashion as in Fig. 6.2. The shaped lines can be cut with the bow saw or keyhole saw (preferably the former) and be finished off with spokeshave and rasp. The straight sides can be sawn away and finished with the plane. To

enable the front and back to be fitted in flush the edges of
the legs are cut as shown in Figs. 6.2 and 6.3. A depth of
22 mm is cut in, this being the thickness of front and
back.

Now proceed with the last-named, cutting them from
22-mm oak to finish 35·5 cm by a trifle over 15 cm. The
ends slope inwards, so that at the top they measure 33

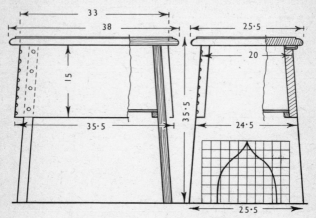

Fig. 6.2 Front and side elevations

All sizes are in centimetres.

cm. In the first place, however, it is better to make the
pieces square. When the edges are trimmed, the simple
gouge-cut decoration can be made at the ends.

As the parts are fixed together with screws, a series of
screw-holes must be bored parallel with the sloping ends.
The screws are recessed as in Fig. 6.4, and the best plan
is first to bore holes large enough to take the screwheads
and passing in about one-third of the thickness. Holes for
the shanks can then be bored.

The parts can now be tried together, and it will be
found that the joints will be a trifle open at one side,

owing to the splay of the side and legs. This necessitates the edges of the notched portion of the legs being planed away at a slight angle. The amount is easily marked with a pencil when the parts are together in position. Afterwards, the whole can be screwed together finally.

The top edges of all the parts will need to be planed to make them level. If left square, they will necessarily slope inwards, owing to the angle of the parts. This is easily done after they are together, since the plane, in resting on the adjacent side, is necessarily held at the required angle. The bottom ends of the legs must be planed similarly. For

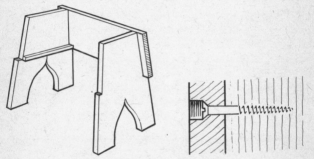

Fig. 6.3 How the parts fit together **Fig. 6.4** Method of recessing the screws

the bottom a piece of 6·5-mm plywood can be used. This is planed so that it can be entered from beneath and be recessed sufficiently for the 12·5-mm fillets to be fixed around as in Figs. 6.2 and 6.3.

The lid is hinged. The moulded edge is an advantage and is easily worked by making first a rebate level with the top square member. It can then be rounded over partly with the smoothing and the rebate planes. The end grain should be done first. Glasspaper held in a hollowed-out rubber will give a good finish. Alternatively, the whole edge can be rounded over. Note that the hinges are

let into the back in their entirety and that the knuckle
projects considerably. If this is done, the lid will open to a
trifle more than a right angle, so that it will remain open.
A pair of chains can be fitted to take the strain if it is
knocked backwards. Finally, the screw-holes can be filled
in with little rounded pieces of oak. This is best done last,
in case it should be necessary to withdraw the screws to
make any adjustment. The whole thing can be stained and
finished with wax.

Cutting List

	Long cm	Wide cm	Thick mm
2 Trestle ends	35	26	22
2 Front and back	36	16	22
1 Top	39	26	22
1 Bottom	30	20	6·5 ply
2 Fillets	30	—	12·5 sq.
2 Fillets	20	—	12·5 sq.

6.2 Long-style Coffee Table

This long-type table has many advantages. It is suitable
for use in front of a settee and is of the right shape to hold
a tray. Furthermore, the available top space is greater
than in the square or circular type without taking up too
much space in the room. The top is of plywood or
blockboard covered with a sheet of plastic laminate. This
could either be of a single piece or it could be made up of
small pieces of plastic sheet assembled in a decorative
design. When small pieces are used, it is essential that all
are the same thickness. The advantage of the plastic
material is that it is both heat- and mark-proof, and is
easily wiped clean.

The framework is unusual in that, although the long

Fig. 6.5 Table handy for the chair-side

side rails are tenoned in the conventional way, the short rails are dovetailed into these long rails as shown in Fig. 6.7. The legs splay in both directions, though the angle is greater in the length than in the width.

Cut out the legs to finish 45 mm at the top, tapering to 25 mm at floor level. Marking out can be done economically by cutting two from a single piece 80 mm

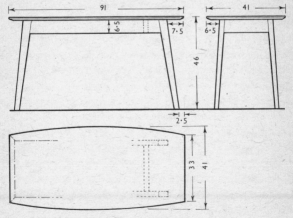

Fig. 6.6 Elevations and plan of table

wide, arranging them top to toe. Clearly the mortises have to be cut at an angle, and if an adjustable bevel is available this can be set to 80 degrees, measuring from the edge to be mortised (not the outside).

Failing the adjustable square, two pieces of thin wood can be nailed together at the required angle for marking and as a guide for mortising. A haunch is cut on the tenon at the top, as shown in Fig. 6.7, and clearly the mortise must be set down from the top accordingly.

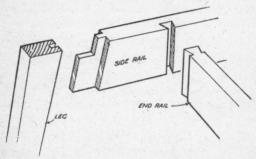

Fig. 6.7 Joints used in the construction of the underframe

The short rails are slot-dovetailed (Fig. 6.7) and, although the slots are cut across square, the rail ends are at an angle of 86 degrees, and the dovetail shoulders, being marked with the gauge, are obviously at the same angle. Try the parts together dry, testing to see that the legs are not in winding. When satisfactory, clean up all surfaces that cannot be cleaned after assembling. Glue each long rail to its pair of legs, cramping and fitting tapered wood blocks beneath the cramp shoes. The glue having set, the joints are levelled and the surfaces cleaned up. Lastly, the dovetailed rails are glued in.

For the top use 12·5-mm multi-ply. Note that an edging is applied all round. The end ones need be only 25 mm wide, but at the sides they must be 75 mm wide to enable the shape to be worked. Fig. 6.8 shows how the edging is fixed with a loose tongue fitting in grooves. The corners can be mitred. Having glued on the edging and levelled the surfaces, the shape is marked along the long sides, a bent lath of wood being used to mark the curve.

Fig. 6.8 Section through table top showing edging

Note that the mitre reaches to the corner after the shape has been cut, and this must be allowed for marking out.

The shape having been cut and cleaned up, the piece of plastic is cut to shape and fixed down with contact adhesive. Afterwards, the underside is bevelled as in Fig. 6.8. No finish is needed on the plastic top, but the framework should be lacquered. Fix the top with pocket screws driven through the rails.

Cutting List

	Long cm	Wide cm	Thick mm
4 Legs	48	5	25
2 Rails	76	7	25
2 Rails	28	7	25
1 Top	88	30	12·5
2 Edgings	93	9	12·5
2 Edgings	36	3·5	12·5

6.3 Small Book Table

The item illustrated in Fig. 6.9 should prove handy to stand by the chair-side in the living room. It is designed so that it can be used from both sides, the top being arranged so that the books can be slid in either side. The lower shelf is handy for magazines and papers. Practically any hardwood could be used, and it is suggested that the plinth be stained a darker shade than the rest. *B*, Fig. 6.9, gives the chief sizes and *C* shows how the parts are joined together.

It will be noticed that the top stands in a trifle and is rounded over. It fits in lapped joints cut in the sides, and these are shown clearly at *C* and *D*. This means that the top must be cut short of the overall length by the thickness of the laps. This might be 4·5 mm, making 9 mm in all. The same applies to the bottom, though this does not project downwards but finishes flush.

Prepare the two sides from 10-mm stuff to finish 43 cm by 46 cm. Plane the edges square and mark out with the gauge and lapped joints. The lap thickness can be 5 mm, and the depth at the top is 14 mm, allowing the rounded edge of the top to stand up 5 mm. At the bottom the depth is 19 mm. Cut the joints by sawing across the grain and chiselling away the waste. A rebate plane is handy with which to finish off. Beneath the top, two rails are dovetailed into the ends as shown at *D*. These are glued in first, after which the four parts are put together with glue and nails, the last-named being punched in and the holes filled up with plastic wood.

The front rail is screwed to the top from beneath. Other pieces running from front to back can also be glued in as shown. These are really glue blocks. They are cut up into lengths of about 4 cm, each with about a 2-mm gap between so that they do not oppose shrinkage. Fillets are

Fig. 6.9 Attractive small book table for the chair-side

    A The complete table
    B Elevations with sizes
    C How the carcase is made
    D Detail of top construction

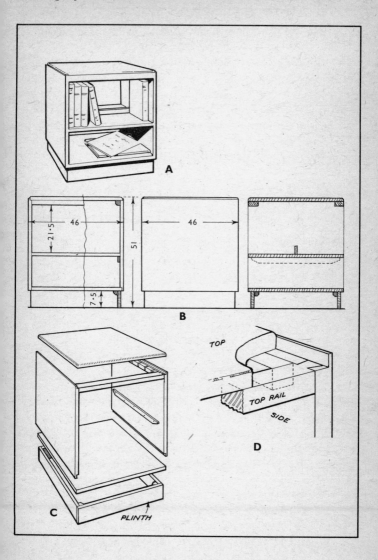

A

B

C PLINTH

D TOP TOP RAIL SIDE

fixed to hold the shelf as at *C*. In the centre of the shelf is
a rail 25 mm high to prevent books from being pushed
too far in. It is screwed from underneath.

A simple way of making the plinth is merely to butt the
corners, glueing and nailing them. Glue blocks in the
corners to strengthen them. To fix the plinth, the table is
turned upside down and the plinth placed in position. A
couple of nails are driven in askew to hold it. Pocket
screws are used to fix it, the holes being generous in size
so that they allow for shrinkage.

Cutting List

	Long cm	Wide cm	Thick mm
2 Sides	44	47	19
1 Top	46	47	19
1 Bottom	46	47	19
1 Shelf	43	47	19
1 Shelf rail	46	3	19
2 Top rails	46	5	19
4 Plinth pieces	46	8	19

Small parts are extra.

6.4. Plant Stand

This makes an attractive and useful item for almost any
room in the house. Its length can be varied to suit any
special space such as a window recess, and the height,
too, can be made to agree with the window. Frequently
such stands are used in showrooms or waiting-rooms,
where short, stubby legs give a suitable height.

It consists of a main box, which is made up complete
in itself, and four separate legs, which are tenoned to
blocks, these in turn being screwed beneath the box. If it
is anticipated that plants are to be watered whilst in the

Fig. 6.10 Plant stand, height of which is variable

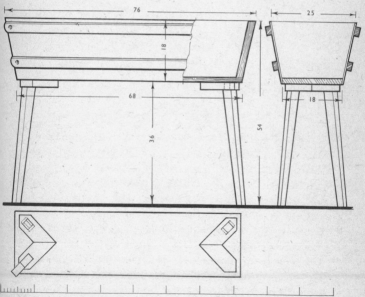

Fig. 6.11 Front and side elevations with scale

box, a metal container can be made to fit inside, but it is not essential if plant pots are merely being stood in the box.

Cut out a bottom to finish 68 cm by 18 cm, planing the edges square. They are then planed at an angle to give the sloping sides. If an adjustable bevel is not available, two strips of wood can be nailed together and used to test the edges to see that the same angle is maintained.

The two ends follow, these being cut and trimmed to the shape given. In this preliminary shaping the edges are planed square, but afterwards the bottom edge should be

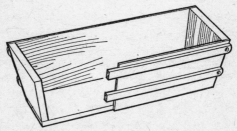

Fig. 6.12 Construction of main box

bevelled to the same angle as the bottom. There is no need to bevel the sides at this stage, as this is more easily done after fixing, though the top edge can be planed to the same angle as the bottom.

Fix the ends with glue and nails, and, when the glue has set, plane the sides to agree with the slope of the bottom. This can be done by allowing the back of the plane to rest on the adjoining edge so that the correct angle is planed automatically. The shape of the sides is ascertained by laying the plywood or hardboard in position and marking round. Fix them with glue and nails and prepare the long rails. These have rounded ends, the length being ascertained by measurement of the box. Fix

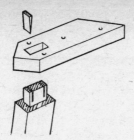

Fig. 6.13 How legs are jointed to blocks

with screws, preferably raisedhead screws fitted into
screw cups.

The legs taper from 38 mm at the top to 22 mm at the
bottom. They can be sawn economically by marking
them side by side, wide end of one against narrow end of
the other. They are tenoned at the top to fit into mortised
blocks, as shown in Fig. 6.13. Since the legs are set at an
angle, the tenons must also be set at an angle to agree.

Blocks are shaped as in the plan in Fig. 6.13. The
mortises run right through and are cut longer at the top
to enable the wedges to force out the tenons and so exert
a dovetail grip. Before assembling, the sharp edges are
rounded over and the legs finally cleaned up. Fix the
blocks with screws as in the plan.

Cutting List

	Long cm	Wide cm	Thick mm
2 Sides	77	19	6·5 ply
2 Ends	19	26	19
2 Rails	77	3·5	19
2 Rails	75	3·5	19
1 Bottom	70	19	19
4 Blocks	16	6	22
4 Legs	38	4·4	22

The finish depends on the woods used and the effect required. One effective way is to polish the legs and blocks black. For this they are stained black and finished with black French polish. For the box portion an attractive treatment is for the long rails to be either lighter or darker than the box itself. The choice depends on the woods. If there is not sufficient contrast, a stain can be used before polishing.

The legs can be marked out economically as described in the article.

6.5 Drop-side Cot

An item of this kind is best made in a plain, straight-grained wood and finished with paint or lacquer. Nursery-rhyme transfers can be added as required. The mattress is the standard 122 cm by 61 cm (4 ft by 2 ft) and can be obtained ready-made, or can be made up from a frame halved or tenoned together and covered with canvas or rubber webbing. Special drop-side fittings are used, and the back is jointed to the sides with the special

Fig. 6.14 Drop-side cot for 122 cm by 61 cm (4 ft by 2 ft) mattress

fittings made for the purpose. The advantage of these is that the cot can be taken to pieces and stacked away flat when not in use.

The main cot parts are made so that the mattress has about 6 mm clearance at ends and back, and about 18

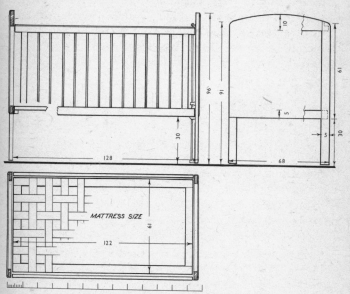

Fig. 6.15 Elevations and plans with main sizes

All sizes are in centimetres.

mm at the front adjoining the drop-front. Begin with the ends. Two rails are needed, the top one being 10 cm wide to enable the curve to be worked. The mortise and tenon joint for this rail is shown in Fig. 6.16. Since the ends of the rail are cut away in sawing the curve, it is clearly necessary to keep the tenon low and to have a wide haunch. The reason for this is made clear from the dotted lines in the elevation in Fig. 6.15. The lower rail has the tenons the full width of the rail.

Glue the parts together and, when set, level the joints. Mark the curve by means of a strip of wood with a nail driven in as centre at one end and with a notch 105 cm away in which a pencil can be held. The waste can be sawn away with the bow saw or, if this is not available, two straight cuts with the hand saw can be made and the final trimming done with the spokeshave or shaper tool.

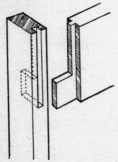   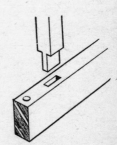

Fig. 6.16 Joint between top side rail and upright

Fig. 6.17 How upright slats are fixed to rails of drop-side

A sheet of plywood or hardboard is trimmed so that it follows the general shape and the edges are rounded over with glasspaper. It is fixed with glue and fine nails. The last-named should be punched in and the holes filled in with putty or other filler.

Back and front frames are identical so far as general construction is concerned. There are two end uprights tenoned into top and bottom rails. They are set in from the ends so that there is space for the rods on which the drop-front slides. Between the uprights are twelve dowels either 9·5 mm or 12·5 mm diameter. They should enter the rails about 12 mm. Above each top rail is a bead rounded at the edges and projecting slightly. These beads look well if in a decorative hardwood left natural colour. They stand in pleasing contrast with the painted finish of the rest of the cot.

The mortises in the rails do not run right through but go in about two-thirds of the distance. The parts are glued together, care being taken to see that the whole is square and free from winding. When the glue has set, the edges are taken off with glasspaper—in fact, all sharp edges and corners should be removed so that there is no danger of the child being injured. In the case of the back, special metal fittings are used to fix it to the ends. At the bottom are two hooks which fit in slotted plates. Threaded hooks are screwed in at the top to the sides, and holes in the top back rails fit over these hooks. Nuts attached to chains are used to keep the back in position. Thus, to take the whole to pieces the nuts are undone and the back lifted straight off.

The drop-front runs on metal rods screwed to the posts

Cutting List

	Long cm	Wide cm	Thick mm
4 Posts	94	5·3	22
2 Side rails	66	10·5	22
2 Side rails	66	5·5	22
2 Panels	70	69	5 ply or hardboard
2 Top rails	128	4·5	22
2 Bottom rails	128	5·5	22
2 Strips	68	—	22 sq.
24 Dowels	51	—	9·5 or 12·5
2 Beads	128	3·5	3·2
2 Mattress sides	128	7	22
2 Mattress ends	63	7	22

of the sides. Holes to fit over these rods must be bored through top and bottom rails at the ends. Pivoted hooks keep the side in the up position. To support the mattress a wood strip is glued and nailed to each end.

Finish the woodwork with three coats of leadless paint, priming, undercoat and final coat. Nursery-rhyme transfers can be added as required.

If rubber webbing is fitted to the mattress it is advisable to fit a centre rail midway along the length. This should be curved downwards in its length so as to allow the rubber webbing to give under the weight. The curve can be cut out of stuff 47·5 mm thick. It can be notched at the ends and screwed to the rails.

6.6 Tea Trolley

The trolley shown in Fig. 6.18 can be used in either the living room or the garden. It has good accommodation, consisting of a top and shelf, and the legs are fitted with 7·5-cm (3-in) castors enabling the trolley to run easily over carpets, etc. Both top and shelf have an edging at back and sides, but the fronts are left clear so that a tray can easily be pushed on. Practically any reliable hardwood could be used, but the top and shelf should match if possible. These are either of plywood, with face veneers, or of blockboard, again veneered. Another alternative which may be easier to obtain is veneered chipboard in 15 mm thickness. Whichever material is used, the front edges should be lipped. Back and sides do not matter since they are concealed.

Prepare the legs to finish 71·5 cm long by 38 mm square. Fix them together temporarily and square across them the positions of the mortises to receive the rails. This ensures their all being marked alike. As shown in Fig. 6.20, the tenons of the rails are set down from the top, and the mortises must, of course, agree. Note also that the top and shelf rest on fillets fixed to the side and back rails, but rest directly on the front rails. This is shown in the sectional side view given in Fig. 6.19. When

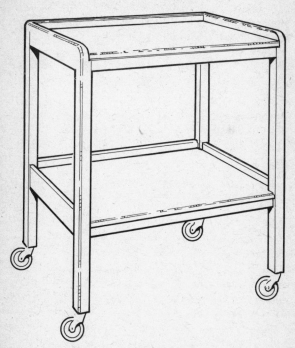

Fig. 6.18 Tea trolley or service waggon 66 cm by 41 cm; height 79 cm overall

all marks have been squared across, the legs can be separated and the lines squared across the adjacent faces where required.

The rails can be dealt with similarly so that corresponding shoulder sizes can be marked exactly. Since all the top rails are flush with the outer surfaces of the legs, the mortise gauge with the same setting can be used throughout. Shelf rails, however, are set in slightly, as shown in Fig. 6.19. Consequently, the mortise gauge will have to be reset by the amount of the set-in for the rails as compared with the legs. Where rails are at the same level, the mortises can meet in the thickness of the legs.

Having fitted all the joints individually, the two sides

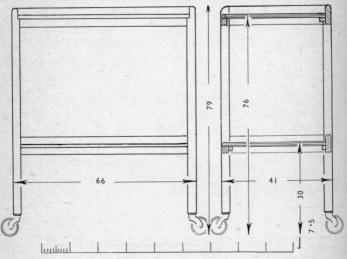

Fig. 6.19 Scale elevations

All sizes are in centimetres.

should be put together independently. When the glue has set, the joints should be levelled and the tops of the legs cut away at the inside level with the rails, as shown in Fig. 6.20. The front corners are then curved and the top edges pencil-rounded, the round dying off as the front curve is reached. Front and back rails now follow, and when the glue has set the inner top back corners of the legs are notched as shown in Fig. 6.20 so that they do not

project into the shelf and top. Finally, top and shelf are
fitted, the front edges being lipped as shown in Fig. 6.20.

An excellent finish for the woodwork is plastic lacquer,
either applied directly to the bare wood or applied
after the latter has first been stained. Better results are

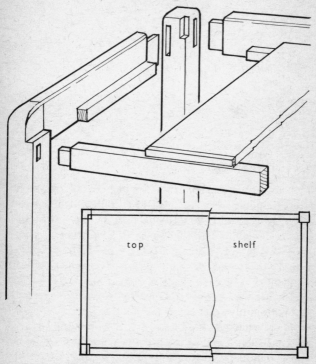

top   shelf

Fig. 6.20 Details of construction and plan views

generally obtained by applying two diluted coats rather
than one coat of full strength.

Incidentally, some may prefer to cover the top and
shelf with plastic laminate rather than to use veneered
ply. This has the advantage of giving a mark-free surface

which is easily cleaned. It could be in natural grain to
match the woodwork, or it could be in a plain contrasting
colour.

Cutting List

	Long cm	Wide cm	Thick mm
4 Legs	75	—	38 sq.
4 End rails	40	7	19
2 Back rails	65	7	19
2 Front rails	65	3	19
2 Top and shelf	63	37	12·5 ply
2 Lippings	63	1·5	5
2 Fillets	62	1·5	15
4 Fillets	37	1·5	15

6.7 Hall Telephone Fitment

This makes a useful and attractive item for the hall. Apart
from enabling the telephonist to sit down, it has a cupboard to hold directories, a drawer for oddments and a
commodious chest in which rugs, blankets, etc., can be
kept. It is largely made in 17-mm veneered chipboard—
mahogany or teak—the advantage of which is its easy
availability in a wide range of sizes. Solid wood is used
for such parts as rails, and for the drawer sides, backs
and bottom plywood is suitable.

Since veneered chipboard has its own characteristics,
the construction has to be specially adapted. Many of the
joints used in solid woodwork would be unsuitable. Furthermore, it is not easy to trim the material to size by
hand methods. Best results are obtained by cutting on the
circular saw dead to size, but if this is impracticable it is
necessary to score right through the veneer with a chisel
or knife at both sides before cutting with the saw; otherwise, the veneer is liable to be splintered off. The saw

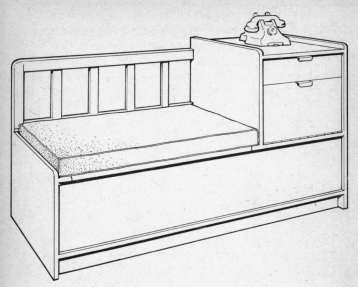

Fig. 6.21 Hall telephone fitment with seat

should have fine teeth and should be used immediately to the waste side of the scored line.

The edge is finally trimmed with the plane, though the edge of the cutter is soon blunted, owing to the abrasive nature of the adhesive with which the chipboard is compressed. Normal shavings cannot be removed, only dust. Some may prefer to use the shaper tool. Where the ready-veneered edges of the chipboard can be retained it is an advantage, but where this is impracticable self-adhesive veneer strips can be used—except on the curved corners of the cupboard, which are best covered with normal veneer cut across the grain to enable it to bend easily. The front edge of the seat has a solid facing tongued on, and in the case of the fall-front of the cupboard an edging of 3-mm solid wood protects the edges of the veneer.

Main sizes in centimetres are given in Figs. 6.22 and 6.23. A slight variation to suit any material that may be available would not matter. Construction is shown in Fig. 6.24. It will be seen that some joints have multiple dowels; others are housed. If preferred, however, either form of joint could be used throughout. The housed joints

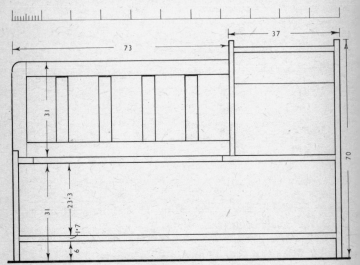

Fig. 6.22 Front elevation with chief sizes

All sizes are in centimetres.

are glued and held with panel pins, either driven in askew at the internal corners after the glue has set or hammered in from outside, punched in and the holes stopped. The advantage of dowels is that no nails are used, but since the holes can only be bored a short way into the thickness of the material, because the screw point of the bit must not penetrate through to the surface, it is necessary to use many dowels to give the necessary strength. It pays to make a special marking-out jig, since it ensures all dowels being exactly in the right positions as well as saving time in individual marking.

Begin by cutting out the right-hand side of the cupboard (*A*, Fig. 6.24). Trim it to size and mark out on the inner side the positions of the various parts. The left-hand

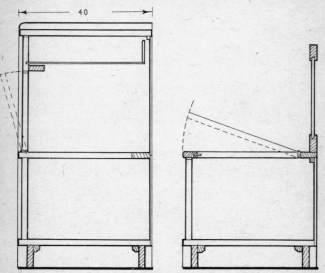

Fig. 6.23 Sectional views through cupboard (*left*) and seat (*right*)

side (*B*) can be marked from it. Where housed joints are used, mark in deeply with chisel and square, cutting right through the veneer, and chisel slightly sloping channels on the waste sides of the lines. These channels enable the saw to be used exactly in the right positions when sawing the sides of the housing. The bulk of the waste can be cut away with a narrow chisel, but the router is needed to bring the housing to even depth. Where

dowels are used, fit a depth gauge to the bit so that
there is no danger of the point of the bit penetrating
right through.

It will be seen that the drawer runners (*K*) are fitted
into housings cut in the sides and are dowelled into the
drawer rail (*J*). Note that the latter stands to the rear of
the drawer front and thus does not show at the front. All

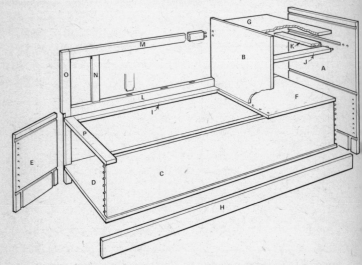

Fig. 6.24 Exploded view showing construction

housings are taken right through to the edges as this
greatly simplifies their cutting. They do not show finally
because the edges are veneered later. Obviously the left-
hand end of the chest (*E*) has to agree exactly with the
right-hand end, and the marking out should be taken
direct from the latter.

Having cut all the joints, each should be fitted
individually, and when satisfactory the inner surfaces
should be cleaned up with fine glasspaper. The main parts

can then be assembled. As in all such cases, it is an
advantage to assemble a few parts at a time, partly
because the job becomes somewhat unmanageable otherwise but also because a large number of cramps would be

Cutting List

			Long cm	Wide cm	Thick mm
A	1 End		71	40·5	17 veneered chipboard
B	1 End		37	40·5	17 ,, ,,
C	1 Front		108	24	17 ,, ,,
D	1 Bottom		109	40	17 ,, ,,
E	1 End		37	40·5	17 ,, ,, or ply
F	1 Bottom		40	35	17 ,, ,,
G	1 Top		36	40·5	17 .. ,,
H	2 Plinths		109	6·5	17 ,, ,,
I	1 Rail		108	6	18 solid
J	1 Rail		35	6	18 ,,
K	2 Runners		32	6	18 ,,
L, M	2 Rails		73	5·5	18 ,,
N	4 Slats		24	4·5	6 ,,
O	1 Upright		65	5·5	18 ,,
P	1 Rail		41	6	18 ,,
	1 Fall-front		35	24	17 veneered chipboard
	1 Drawer front		35	11	17 ,, ,,
	1 Drawer back		34	7	9·5 ply
	2 Drawer sides		38	9	9·5 ,,
	1 Drawer bottom		35	36	5 ,,
	1 Chest back		108	28	6·5 ,,
	1 Cupboard back		35	38	6·5 ,,

Some sizes will have to be adapted to suit the widths of lippings used.
Also to suit the use of dowels or house joints.

needed if many were put together at the same time. First,
cupboard bottom (*F*) is tongued or dowelled to back rail
(*I*), the latter in turn being dowelled or tenoned to end rail
(*P*). This makes a complete assembly and should be set

aside for the glue to set. Now screw bottom (*D*) to front
(*C*) and add the two to ends (*A*) and (*E*), at the same time
slipping in assembly (*F*), (*I*), (*P*). When the glue has set,
plinth (*H*) and the corresponding rear item can be glued
in, glue blocks being afterwards rubbed in at the internal
angles to strengthen the joints. Inner end (*B*), top (*G*) and
drawer rails (*J*) follow. Runners (*K*) can be added after
the whole has set.

A separate framework is made up for the seat back. It
consists of two rails (*M*) and (*L*) tenoned or dowelled to
upright (*O*) with slats (*N*) stub-tenoned in. Note that
upright (*O*) is notched where it joins end (*E*). The easiest
way of assembling is to glue the slats to the two rails, add
the upright and leave to set. The joints are levelled and
the whole slipped into the main assembly. Fillets are
glued and nailed around the inside of the cupboard and
chest to give a fixing for the plywood backs. They are not
needed at the bottom of either cupboard or chest as the
bottoms stand in at the rear, the backs being fitted to the
back edge.

It is advisable to tongue a solid piece to the front edge
of the chest top as shown in Fig. 6.23. If it is made to
stand up a trifle above the main veneered surface, it
simplifies the later cleaning up. Its front edge is pencil-
rounded at both edges. In the case of the fall-front of the
cupboard, the lippings need be only 3 mm thick. Here
again, they should be a trifle proud of the surface to
enable them to be levelled down to the veneered surface
later. Piano-type hinges are used at the bottom and a
slotted stay is fitted to limit the movement of the fall. The
simplest construction for the drawer is that shown on
page 86, except that the front projects downwards so that
it stands in front of the drawer rail.

An excellent finish is plastic lacquer diluted to half
strength with thinners. Two coats may be needed, after

which the whole can be finished with wax polish. Finally,
a loose squab cushion is made for the seat.

*　　*　　*

*It may be a platitude that to finish well is better than to
start well, but it is absolutely true about woodwork. Look
at that last thing you made and see if it isn't!*

Index